ROOTED:NEW TESTAMENT

table of contents

ROOTED:NEW TESTAMENT

A PERSONAL NOTE FROM DOUG FIELDS . . .

Welcome to Rooted: New Testament! It is my prayer that this resource is more than simply a blessing for your ministry. As Paul admonished Timothy to "excel still more," this material will lengthen and strengthen the spiritual foundation of your students. My Saddleback Church colleague, Matt McGill, has invested a lot of time researching and teaching the material you have in your hands. It's thorough and relevant, but most of all . . . life-changing.

One of the great joys of my life is working with Matt. I was his youth pastor many years ago and he has definitely surpassed me in many ways. I have great spiritual pride in his intelligence, leadership, and character. Several years ago, Matt came to me and asked a simple question: "Doug, what is it that you really want to see happen in our youth ministry, but you don't have the time to develop?" What a great question! I told Matt that there are always some students who have a deep hunger for more knowledge and Bible information, and that I wished I had the time to create something that was more than a Bible study . . . more like a Rooted: New Testament.

bingo! that's where it started.

I sketched out on a napkin the classes I thought would be vital, and Matt was off to the races. As he developed the material, we would bat around the content and talk about it's relevance to teenagers. But you should know this from the outset: I am a minor contributor to this work. Matt is the main voice and teacher of this material in the Student Ministry at Saddleback Church.

The main reason behind my excitement for creating this material is the simple fact that many students head off to Bible college or a local university thinking they're spiritually prepared to handle all that comes their way. The truth is, you and I both know that a much-higher-than-we-like percentage of students "graduate from God" when they graduate from high school. Part of the reason why the drop-out rate is so high is an inadequate knowledge base on the essentials of the faith. While we like to think our flock knows how to feed themselves, life and college are filled with people all-too-ready to knock the spoon out of their hands before it reaches their lips. This material, combined with your aggressive shepherding of the souls God has entrusted to you, will give each student who completes this course the discernment to know when the wrong person is reaching for their "spiritual fork," and the intellectual strength to personally—and appropriately—knock that arm away when it gets too close.

Where should you best teach this material? At Saddleback, we've taught this material in several formats. We've had success...
- on weekend retreats,
- as a Sunday School class,
- in the evenings at a home,
- in a Saturday morning seminar format, and even (believe it or not)
- allowing students to read through it on their own and study it themselves.

We've discovered that three to four hour blocks of time (for each lesson) are the best way for the student to absorb the material and answer the questions you hope will come your way. Currently, however, we are teaching this on Sunday mornings in hour-long Sunday school sessions, where each lesson can last several weeks. It's taught as an elective for those students who want something different and deeper than they are experiencing during our "typical" Sunday morning outreach program.

As you will see, this material is for students who are serious about learning and those who are filled with questions. And speaking of answering questions, I'm going to let Matt pick it up from here to answer a few questions that you may have.

some thoughts before you use Rooted: New Testament [from matt mcgill]

Some leaders wonder whether their students, even two or three in their group, will be up for the challenge of going deeper in the Bible. For anything worthwhile, there will be a cost. For you the teacher, the cost is time in preparation. But that is a small price to pay for the benefits I've been able to witness in our ministry.

To name a few:
1. Their understanding—not just knowledge—of the Bible will increase.
2. With your enthusiastic teaching, their love for God's Word will grow.
3. They will be better equipped to answer honest questions from those the Holy Spirit might be drawing to the Father.
4. They will be "ready to defend" their faith, and have intelligent conversations in an antagonistic academic culture, an ambivalent work culture, and an amoral party culture.

As you can see, this resource contains a ton of material. Each lesson took us about three hours to teach, and most of the time we weren't able to finish all of the material. With six lessons, you have at least 18 hours of material.

Why so much material?

I'd rather give you "too much" content, letting you cut and edit to fit your student's needs and your own time constraints. The alternative would be leaving you short, and putting you into a position where you have to create new lessons on your own.

Understanding the Purpose of Rooted: New Testament

No one needs to tell you that youth workers have a unique opportunity to make an impact in the lives of students at a critical moment in their development. Unfortunately, students graduate from our ministries and often enter hostile arenas. They are bombarded with different lifestyles, ideas, and beliefs. They also form relationships with people who are passionate about lies concerning God's character, His plan, the authority of the Bible, the relevancy of the church, and the whole attitude that being a Christian may not be the easiest thing, but it's the right thing. As caring shepherds, we don't like to see our flock wander into barren pastures where they could buy into false beliefs. Building a love for the right nourishment will give them a solid foundation that will help prepare them for what is to come.

Although "youth ministry" (as we know it) didn't exist in Paul's day, it's still no wonder that he gave us this warning:

So then, just as you received Christ Jesus as Lord, continue to live in him, rooted and built up in him, strengthened in the faith as you were taught, and overflowing with thankfulness. See to it that no one takes you captive through hollow and deceptive philosophy, which depends on human tradition and the basic principles of this world rather than on Christ (Colossians 2:6-8).

Whether a graduate goes into the work place, a Christian college, or a secular university, they're going to have their ears tickled with strange philosophies. Some of what they hear will sound good and seem to make sense. They'll be challenged with good questions. But because these questions will often come from people who haven't searched the Bible for the Truth, the answers may not be complete.

No youth leader wants a student to know half an answer to important questions like:
- Would a loving God really "send" people to hell?
- Isn't the God of the Old Testament different than the one in the New Testament?
- Did Jesus really claim to be God, or was it something His disciples made up?
- Everyone has their own interpretation of the Bible, so why can't mine be just as right as yours?

And, of course, the inevitable:
- If God is a God of love, why do people suffer?

I could go on, but you know that outside answers to these kinds of questions will come in the form of "hollow and deceptive" philosophies to which many students are susceptible.

Among many other goals, these are some of the issues and reasons why this resource was created. Combine this material with your own, couple it with prayer and a close relationship with your students, and you'll be able to reach these goals in a manner that is best suited to your ministry context.

Let me boil down the benefits of Rooted: New Testament into three succinct goals:
1. Communicate Essential Biblical Truths
As an educational resource, Rooted: New Testament exists to communicate some of the important faith truths that God has revealed in His Word.

2. Give Students An Exciting Overview of the Bible
Your students will get a taste of individual books in the Bible that will make them salivate for more. It will give them the "I can do the Bible" feel that any mature believer needs to have in order to feed themselves—and hear from the Holy Spirit the rest of their lives.

Have you ever just flipped through your Bible, stopped at a random place to start reading? While I don't want to criticize this demonstration of faith in the Holy Spirit's leading, I believe equipping a student to be more intentional in their devotions or personal study of God's Word has value.

3. Improve Bible Study Skills
Any leader knows how difficult it is to read the Bible—and understand it—without a working knowledge of the historical context of each book. This material will give practical tools and thorough training to help them read God's Word with understanding.

some helpful tips for teaching this material

1. Take Time to Prep!
Hopefully, this resource will drastically cut down the time you'd need to teach this material. Of course, you'll still need to prepare on your own so you can . . .
(a) make sure you understand the material (it's often difficult to teach someone else's material!)
(b) think about what questions your students will ask (and look for subjects to delve into deeper with your own questions)
(c) decide which things you'll want to emphasize (and which things you'll want to gloss over).

Please note: Each lesson in this resource is basically a huge outline, and to teach this material well, you'll need to expand on the material quite often to make it understandable for your students.

2. Encourage Discussion and Questions
Since Rooted: New Testament covers A LOT of material, usually the best way to communicate this is in a lecture format. Unfortunately, lecturing can be boring so do all you can to NOT let this get in the way of your students learning. If there is a point that seems especially confusing or interesting, take time to unpack it with your students. Encourage them to stop you if they have questions or something important to say.

There were several times when I was teaching these lessons that I didn't finish the material because I felt that it was more important to "pull off the road" and "camp" at a particular point for a while.

With this being said, it's important that you keep everyone on topic . . . or at least close! You've prepped a good lesson, so be a teacher and move your students through the material. Just because a student wants to talk about something that doesn't mean their topic is worthwhile. Some questions don't need to take everyone's time to deal with, so use discernment as to what's the highway, and what's a rabbit trail.

Here's how I typically handle questions: If a question is on topic, or relatively close, I'll throw the question out to the rest of the group to get their input. I carefully nudge here and there, asking different flavors of the same question to move the group to answer the question on their own. I've found that the material gets planted deeper in their hearts if they're the ones doing the digging. Warning: there are some students who like to dominate. It could be that they just know more, or that they have a need to appear spiritual. Either way, it won't be healthy for the group to let this happen too often. If the student heads into a long monologue, politely ask that person to summarize what he or she is trying to say in a few sentences. If a question is way off topic, I'll quickly give "my answer" and/or tell the student he or she's a little off topic and promise to meet afterward.

3. Create Homework Assignments
I probably wouldn't call any assignments "homework," but as you work through the material, be on the lookout for great quiet-time exercises your students can do on their own. Like Bible college, the tendency will be to view God's Word as a textbook instead of life-giving spiritual sustenance. Address this fact with them, and encourage them to spend time daily with the Father.

4. Determine a Framework and Schedule Timing That Works for Your Ministry

When I originally taught this material, we planned for THREE HOURS and worked through an entire lesson. Even with breaks, many students don't want to commit to something that is almost as long as a baseball game. Depending on your teaching style, and how you decide to teach Rooted: New Testament, you should consider a time frame that works best for your own life, as well as the time constraints of those interested enough to attend.

We have provided the Rooted: New Testament for you in a digital format so you can change anything along the way. For sections you don't want to cover, fill in the blanks on the student workbooks and skip over them when you're teaching the lesson. You could say, "We're going to skip over page xx, but I left it in your notes in case you want to read it on your own."

5. Go Beyond the Blanks

I find that fill-in sentences are helpful when using lecture format, but they are not without some problems or without a lot of teasing from Doug who calls me "blank happy." As a teacher, it can be easy to simply walk through the blanks and offer little other material such as further explanations, illustrations, or stories. As a learner, it's possible for students to get so caught up in simply writing things down that they forget to keep their mind engaged. To guard against this, when I get to an especially important point I'll say something like, "Okay, look up here for a moment and forget the notes. Get those synapses firing and see if you can wrap your mind around this . . . "

6. Don't Wander Too Far From the Practical

When it comes to teaching a lot of information, sometimes it's easy to get caught up in the details. We get excited about facts and trivia and forget about the practical implications. I love the details of the Bible and find them fascinating, but it's essential to keep things grounded in reality. I once had a seminary professor tell me I was too practical for seminary. (That was one of the highlights of my life, because Doug couldn't believe it—he was telling me just the opposite!)

God has entrusted us with a treasure: our students. The Great Commission tells us to "teach them to obey" (Matthew 28:20), not teach them a ton of useless facts. When I was teaching about the hot topic of the fall of Samaria, I stopped working through the notes and said, "If God can use the Assyrians for his purposes, what does this mean for your life?" Impressed with his own wit, one student said, "Well, the way you describe the Assyrians reminds me of my Math teacher . . . " Although this was funny for the moment, I brought it back to the practical and asked, "How is God moving things in your life to get your attention? Are you tempted to think that God can only work through the Church or our programs?"

Without good preparation, this kind of thinking can be difficult, especially because it means struggling personally with God's Word. Discerning practicality for your students will take some time, but I want to challenge you to discover how you ought to specifically encourage your students to live in obedience to God's Word.

Thanks for taking a chance with this material. As always, Doug wants the last word. Back to you Doug.

[from doug fields]

Trust me, Matt wasn't too practical for seminary, but he was paying attention. Matt is a thinker, a lover of God's Word, a great youth worker, and a best friend. If some of this material is too heady for you, you can join my club. Unlike most of Simply Youth Ministry's material, this isn't our typical (1) open the document and (2) start teaching. There are a few suggestions if you think it's too much work for you:

(a) Find a Bible teacher in your church who could digest the material and teach it for you.

(b) Give it to a spiritually mature teenager to read it, study it, and then teach it.

(c) Read it with a few students as a notebook. Stop and start as often as you want. It doesn't have to be taught, it can be read and discussed.

(d) Write Matt an email and encourage him to teach it on a DVD so you can show it to your students. But, don't hold your breath—took over five years for Matt to put this in printed form. I wrote about Rooted: New Testament in the *Purpose Driven Youth Ministry* book in 1999, and we didn't make it available until 2004.

Thank you for your commitment to God, God's Word, and the students and families in your church. May you be blessed as you attempt to take students to a deeper knowledge of God's Word.

Blessings,

Doug Fields

INTRODUCTION TO THE BIBLE

ROOTED:NEW TESTAMENT

ROOTED:NEW TESTAMENT

study one introduction to the Bible

TABLE OF CONTENTS

WHAT KIND OF BOOK IS THIS?

1. The Bible is **mostly history**.

2. The Bible is **much more** than history.

   (a) It's really God's **autobiography**.

   (b) This means it's a combination of the facts of history and the heart of God for all mankind. It's His plan of how He created, sustains, works in, and saves the world.

3. The Bible is a book about God's **love affai**r with people, His most unique creation.

   (a) John said, "God is love" (1 John 4:8). If this is His character, then everything He does is out of love for His creation.

   (b) God's love includes everyone (John 3:16).

   (c) His character doesn't change (James 1:17).

4. Because the Bible demonstrates God's love for His people, it is called **salvation** history.

> **SALVATION HISTORY:**
> This term refers to the series of historical events that are specific acts of God to save His people.

SALVATION HISTORY 101

   (a) Adam and Eve were created perfect (very good);

   (b) Adam fell into sin, and consequently, away from God;

   (c) God used the Jews to bring His chosen Messiah into the world to save the world, not just the Jews.

5. The Bible is different from a **history** textbook; the Bible is didactic, influencing how we live.

   (a) It was written to **change** your life.

   Possible discussion question:

   How can words on a page change a person?

   (b) If you open your **heart**, it will!

   Possible discussion questions:

   What does it mean to "open your heart"?

   Why is having an open heart so important to change?

   How does a Christian keep an open heart?

6. Why else did God **write** the Bible?

   To give people wisdom about life and to bring people **closer** to Him.

   Possible discussion questions:

   Why should wisdom be valuable to our lives?

   What are the different ways it is acquired?

   Does everyone acquire wisdom the same way?

   What are God's ways for passing along wisdom?

[the uniqueness of the Bible]

1. Common myth: the Bible is just another "**religious**" book.

2. Facts about the Bible that make it incredibly unique:

(a) Written over a **2,000**-year span.

(b) Written by more than **40** authors, from all walks of life—educated and uneducated, Jews and Gentiles. Most of them didn't know each other.

Moses: **politician/shepherd**

Peter: **fisherman**

Amos: **herdsman**

Joshua: **general**

Luke: **doctor**

Solomon: **king**

Matthew: **tax collector**

Paul: **pharisee and tent maker**

(c) Written in different **moods** (from times of joy to the depths of sadness).

(d) Written in **three** different languages.

Daniel 2:20 (Aramaic)

Praise be to the name of God for ever and ever; wisdom and power are his.

עָנֵה דָנִיֵּאל וְאָמַר לֶהֱוֵא שְׁמֵהּ דִּי־אֱלָהָא מְבָרַךְ

מִן־עָלְמָא וְעַד־עָלְמָא דִּי חָכְמְתָא וּגְבוּרְתָא דִּי לֵהּ־הִיא:

Deuteronomy 6:4 (Hebrew)

"Hear, O Israel: The Lᴏʀᴅ our God, the Lᴏʀᴅ is one."

שְׁמַע יִשְׂרָאֵל יְהוָה אֱלֹהֵינוּ יְהוָה ׀ אֶחָד:

John 3:16 (Greek)

"For God so loved the world that He gave his one and only Son, that whoever believes in him shall not perish but have eternal life."

Οὕτως γὰρ ἠγάπησεν ὁ θεὸς τὸν κόσμον, ὥστε τὸν υἱὸν τὸν μονογενῆ ἔδωκεν,
ἵνα πᾶς ὁ πιστεύων εἰς αὐτὸν μὴ ἀπόληται ἀλλ᾽ ἔχῃ ζωὴν αἰώνιον.

3. The Bible contains hundreds of **controversial** issues, but there is one unfolding story: God's love for His people and His work to draw them closer to Him through Jesus Christ. It can truly be said that because of the prophetic elements throughout the Old Testament, the whole Bible is about Jesus.

4. Although there's GREAT diversity (i.e. voices of authority, two covenants, different styles of literature, different languages, different readers and situations, different moods and tones, etc.) in the Bible, there is GREATER unity (i.e. consistent moral message, prophecies don't conflict with one another, theological themes are consistent, moral teachings are the same, and many others). How did this happen?

5. The Bible was written by the **Holy Spirit**!

All Scripture is God-breathed and is useful for teaching . . . so that the man of God may be thoroughly equipped for every good work (2 Timothy 3:16-17).

If God's love letter was written with great diversity and even greater unity to give us wisdom for life and to draw us closer to Him . . . then isn't it worth our attention?

[the structure of the Bible]

1. The Bible isn't just one book. It's a collection of **many** books.

2. The Bible has two major divisions.

   (a) Old Testament: has **39** books.

   (b) New Testament: has **27** books.

> **OLD TESTAMENT:**
> People have access to God through the priesthood.

> **NEW TESTAMENT:**
> People have access to God through Jesus.

What should we call the two parts of the Bible, Testament or Covenant?

Testament is usually used in terms of a person's "last will and testament," and determines what happens to property after death. New Testament people have access to God through Jesus.

Covenant is "an agreement between two people or two groups that involves promises on the part of each to the other."

When speaking of the Bible, the Old and New Testament are better understood as the Old and New Covenant. The agreement between God and His people is different between the Old and the New. But God does not change. What changes, is how we relate to God. (See Hebrews 8:8-12.)

---

3. The divisions of the Old Testament:

   - **Torah** or Pentateuch

     Written by Moses regarding creation, the beginnings of the nation of Israel, and the Law.

> **TORAH:**
> Hebrew word meaning law, instruction, or commandment.

   - **History**

     About the rise, fall, captivity, and return of the nation of Israel.

   - **Poetry** and Wisdom

     All from different time periods, but written mainly by David and Solomon.

   - **Prophets**

     Called "major" and "minor," not due to importance, but simply the size of the books.

4. The divisions of the New Testament:

- Gospels and **Acts**

  About the life, teachings, and work of Jesus and the early church.

- **Letters**

  Various letters written to a particular audience or person, usually for a specific purpose.

- **Revelation**

  Prophecy is such a big deal it gets its own category!

5. The Old Testament divisions and their books:

TORAH	HISTORY	POETRY & WISDOM	PROPHETS	
Genesis	Joshua	Job	Isaiah	Jonah
Exodus	Judges	Psalms	Jeremiah	Micah
Leviticus	Ruth	Proverbs	Lamentations	Nahum
Numbers	1 & 2 Samuel	Ecclesiastes	Ezekiel	Habakkuk
Deuteronomy	1 & 2 Kings	Song of Songs	Daniel	Zephaniah
	1 & 2 Chronicles		Hosea	Haggai
	Ezra		Joel	Zechariah
	Nehemiah		Amos	Malachi
	Esther		Obadiah	

6. The New Testament divisions and their books:

GOSPELS AND ACTS	LETTERS		REVELATION
Matthew	Romans	Titus	Revelation
Mark	1 & 2 Corinthians	Philemon	
Luke	Galatians	Hebrews	
John	Ephesians	James	
Acts	Philippians	1 & 2 Peter	
	Colossians	1, 2, & 3 John	
	1 & 2 Thessalonians	Jude	
	1 & 2 Timothy		

7. The verse and chapter numbers in the Bible are not inspired, or directed, by the Holy Spirit. They were added by a monk in the Middle Ages, not by God. (And though the chapters and verses are not always in good places, they are useful for reference and study.)

INSPIRATION: HOW THE BIBLE WAS WRITTEN

1. The Bible came to us through the **inspiration** of the Holy Spirit.

   - No person can ever see God on his or her own. They need to be **shown**.

   No one has ever seen God, but God the One and Only, who is at the Father's side, has made him known (John 1:18).

2. The Bible was written by God **through** people. This miracle is called "inspiration."

3. Although God has revealed Himself in many ways, the most significant way is through **Jesus** (Hebrews 1:1-3).

4. Our knowledge about Jesus comes from the Bible, so what we share with others about our faith includes truth from the Bible to give it **authority**.

5. Each biblical author expressed the Word of God out of His own experience:

   (a) personality

   (b) language and grammar

   (c) historical **context**

Q: If humans are imperfect, how could they write a perfect Bible?

WHO WROTE THAT?
The Gospel of Luke was written by a doctor. Because of that, he uses many technical medical terms the other three books do not include.

6. Because the Scriptures are God-breathed (2 Timothy 3:16), there are no **mistakes**.

Above all, you must understand that no prophecy of Scripture came about by the prophet's own interpretation. For prophecy never had its origin in the will of man, but men spoke from God as they were carried along by the Holy Spirit (2 Peter 1:20-21).

So What's the Big Deal About Inspiration?

Since the Bible is inspired by God there are no errors. It is the ultimate authority for the truth about God and His eternal plan.

This means that when there is a conflict between:

- my feelings and the Bible . . . the Bible wins;
- my intellectual conclusions, opinions, and human reason and the Bible . . . the Bible wins;
- my personal experiences and the Bible . . . the Bible wins.

THERE IS NO CONTEST WHEN SOMEONE OR SOMETHING TRIES TO GO AGAINST THE BIBLE!

Scripture is:

- **Authoritative** for truth: includes theology, doctrine, and morality.

- **Universal**: spans across all cultures and time.

- **Sacred**: holy and inspired from God.

- **Normative**: for ALL believers and the rest of the world.

CANON:
This term comes from the Hebrew word for reed. A reed was straight and often used to measure things.

CANONIZATION: HOW THE BIBLE WAS RECOGNIZED

Now that we know the Bible is a collection of books, how did they get collected? Who chose them? Why did they make the decision to include them in the Bible?

THE BIBLE:
A collection of inspired books.

The bigger question is: What qualifies as Scripture and what does not?

The Importance of Canon

As Christians, having the Bible is of the utmost importance. Without God's many revelations that were written down, His acts would be forgotten, misunderstood, or passed over. Without supernatural revelation, the death of Jesus would have just been another terrible evil the Roman Empire committed. Canon is the process of the Church recognizing God's true revelations as Scripture.

1. The process of canonization involves two parties:

The **author**.

The **Church** (or the people of God).

2. The author writes the Scripture through the inspiration of the Holy Spirit.

3. The Church recognizes (or "canonizes") the Scripture through the revelation of the Holy Spirit. (God communicating truth, revealing that which was previously unknown.)

4. A book is canonized as Scripture based upon the evidence of inspired authorship.

IMPORTANT: The Church did not create the Canon or the Bible, but only recognized that which was already Scripture.

5. The first part to canonization is the actual writing of a book. It is simple: God worked through imperfect people to bring us His **perfect** message.

6. The second part is a bit more complicated, and the process **differs** between the Old Testament and the New Testament.

What is that evidence? What are the criteria that must be met for a book to be "put" into the Bible?

[old testament canon]

1. There is not a lot of **detailed** information about how Old Testament books were canonized. What we do know is that a near-complete version of the Old Testament was in circulation about 200 years before the birth of Christ.

2. However, there are many sources that tell us the Old Testament is Canon. While we may not know exactly how it was canonized, we do know that the process **did happen**.

3. Old Testament Canon happened in three waves or stages:
First: Law—5 books

Second: Prophets—8 books

Third: Writings—11 books

Organization of the Hebrew Bible

The Hebrew Bible is organized much differently from our English version. They have three divisions:

TORAH: Genesis, Exodus, Leviticus, Numbers, Deuteronomy

PROPHETS: Joshua, Judges, 1 & 2 Samuel, 1 & 2 Kings, Isaiah, Jeremiah, Ezekiel, Hosea, Joel, Amos, Obadiah, Jonah, Micah, Nahum, Habbakkuk, Zephaniah, Haggai, Zechariah, Malachi

SACRED WRITINGS: Psalms, Proverbs, Ruth, Job, Song of Songs, Lamentations, Ecclesiastes, Esther, Daniel, Ezra, Nehemiah, 1 & 2 Chronicles.

4. The Old Testament Canon starts with **Moses**.

- Moses **received** the Law (Ten Commandments and then some) from God.

At that time I stood between the Lord and you to declare to you the word of the Lord, because you were afraid of the fire and did not go up the mountain (Deuteronomy 5:5).

- Moses **wrote** them down.

Then the Lord said to Moses, "Write down these words, for in accordance with these words I have made a covenant with you and with Israel." Moses was there with the Lord forty days and forty nights without eating bread or drinking water. And he wrote on the tablets the words of the covenant—the Ten Commandments (Exodus 34:27-28).

- The people accepted his writings as **authoritative**.

Go near and listen to all that the Lord our God says. Then tell us whatever the Lord our God tells you. We will listen and obey (Deuteronomy 5:27).

5. Jesus said the Old Testament was **Scripture**.

He said to them, "This is what I told you while I was still with you: Everything must be fulfilled that is written about me in the Law of Moses, the Prophets and the Psalms" (Luke 24:44).

"And so upon you will come all the righteous blood that has been shed on earth, from the blood of righteous Abel to the blood of Zechariah son of Berekiah, whom you murdered between the temple and the altar" (Matthew 23:35).

Abel to Zechariah

Remember, the Bible that Jesus used was organized differently. Chronicles was the last book in this Bible. When he quotes Abel to Zechariah, he is talking about the ENTIRE Old Testament. Abel is in the first book, and Zechariah was in the last book.

6. The New Testament calls the Old Testament:

- Scripture (John 10:35; 19:36)

- the Scriptures (Matthew 22:29; Acts 18:24)

- Holy Scriptures (Romans 1:2)

- sacred writings (2 Timothy 3:15)

- law (John 10:34; 12:34; 15:25; 1 Corinthians 14:21)

- law and the prophets (Matthew 5:17; 7:12; 22:40; Luke 16:16; 24:44)

> **EXTRA-BIBLICAL:**
> This term applies to any text that is not the Bible. Often these sources help to illuminate or explain portions of the Bible. For example, Josephus, a Jewish historian from the time of Jesus has recorded many cultural insights that aren't found in the Bible.

7. The bottom line is this: Jesus and the rest of the New Testament authors referred to the entire Old Testament as **Scripture**.

[new testament canon]

1. There were basically four criteria the early church fathers used to determine the canonicity of New Testament texts:

- **Content** (Is the book consistent with the Gospels, and the OT?)

- **Authorship** (Was the author an Apostle or did he have a sustained relationship with an Apostle?)

- **Catholicity** (Was it universally accepted by churches?)

- **Spiritual** (Does this material reveal the truth of God? Is the book spiritual in character?)

2. In the early church, about 180 A.D., elders from cities where the Church was strong, met and decided which letters in their possession had Apostolic credibility. These men of God **collected**, evaluated, and decided which of the books would be considered Christian Scripture.

3. Summary of canon:

"Jesus Himself affirmed the full authority of the Old Testament as Scripture. Then He made His own words and deeds equally authoritative, and promised the apostles that the Holy Spirit would remind them of His ministry and teach them its significance. The canon of the New Testament, then, is the authoritative record and interpretation of God's revelation of Himself through Jesus Christ." (R. Gundry. A Survey of the New Testament, p. 58)

[what about the stuff that didn't get in?]

1. Not **everything** made it into the Bible.

> **APOSTLE:**
> Someone who had actually seen or been with Jesus, and then personally commissioned by Him to carry the message of the Gospel.

2. Some of the material that didn't make it into the Canon can be found in the Apocrypha (definition: "hidden").

   - These books were written **in-between** the Old Testament and the New Testament. A time of about 400 years.

3. The Apocrypha was a part of the Bible called the Septuagint (abbreviated LXX).

   - LXX means **70**.

   - The LXX was a common **translation** used during Jesus' time.

   - The LXX was written in **Greek**, which was the language everyone knew.

> **COMMUNICATION:**
> Communication and transportation were limited when the Bible was written and recognized as canon. It's interesting that the churches who had little or no contact often reached similar conclusions about which texts were Scripture.

4. Why is the Apocryphal literature not in the Protestant Bible?

   - Jesus, the Apostles, and the first generation of church fathers after the Apostles never referred to any passage in the Apocrypha in their writings, nor did they ever refer to it as Scripture.

   - The Jews do not consider the Apocrypha to be Scripture.

5. The Apocrypha is in Roman Catholic Bibles, but is not considered to be on the same **level** as the "rest" of Scripture.

ILLUMINATION: HOW THE BIBLE IS UNDERSTOOD

1. We cannot fully understand the Bible without faith in Jesus as our **Savior**.

   - Why? We need the Holy Spirit to **teach** us what would otherwise be impossible to understand.

For who among men knows the thoughts of a man except the man's spirit within him? In the same way no one knows the thoughts of God except the Spirit of God. We have not received the spirit of the world but the Spirit who is from God, that we may understand what God has freely given us. This is what we speak, not in words taught us by human wisdom but in words taught by the Spirit, expressing spiritual truths in spiritual words. The man without the Spirit does not accept the things that come from the Spirit of God, for they are foolishness to him, and he cannot understand them, because they are spiritually discerned. "For who has known the mind of the Lord that he may instruct him?" But we have the mind of Christ (1 Corinthians 2:11-14,16).

"But when he, the Spirit of truth, comes, he will guide you into all truth" (John 16:13).

2. Anyone can be a Christian, so anyone can **understand** the Bible. (It does not take a degree from a Bible college to understand Scripture.)

3. Illumination is the Holy Spirit's work of making **truth** from the Bible clear when a Christian reads the Bible. This is why people are touched differently by the same passages. The Holy Spirit always teaches us what we need to know, when we need to know it. This doesn't mean the Bible is only a matter of interpretation, and that any verse can mean anything. God is consistent in the overall meaning of Scripture, but is creative and powerful enough to make it apply to various people's circumstances in different places in the world at every point of history.

EIGHT IMAGES THE BIBLE USES TO DESCRIBE ITSELF

1. **Seed**
For you have been born again, not of perishable seed, but of imperishable, through the living and enduring word of God (1 Peter 1:23).

2. <u>Sword</u>

Take the helmet of salvation and the sword of the Spirit, which is the word of God (Ephesians 6:17).

For the word of God is living and active. Sharper than any double-edged sword, it penetrates even to dividing soul and spirit, joints and marrow; it judges the thoughts and attitudes of the heart (Hebrews 4:12).

- In Ephesians the sword is in our hand, defending against the enemy.

- In Hebrews the sword is in God's hands, penetrating and deeply impacting our lives.

3. <u>Food</u>

When your words came, I ate them; they were my joy and my heart's delight, for I bear your name, O Lᴏʀᴅ God Almighty (Jeremiah 15:16).

Jesus answered, "It is written: 'Man does not live on bread alone, but on every word that comes from the mouth of God' " (Matthew 4:4).

4. <u>Milk</u>

Like newborn babies, crave pure spiritual milk, so that by it you may grow up in your salvation (1 Peter 2:2).

5. <u>Hammer</u>

"Is not my word like fire," declares the Lᴏʀᴅ, "and like a hammer that breaks a rock in pieces?" (Jeremiah 23:29).

6. <u>Fire</u>

Therefore this is what the Lᴏʀᴅ God Almighty says: "Because the people have spoken these words, I will make my words in your mouth a fire and these people the wood it consumes" (Jeremiah 5:14).

7. <u>Lamp</u>

Your word is a lamp to my feet and a light for my path (Psalm 119:105).

8. **Mirror**

Anyone who listens to the word but does not do what it says is like a man who looks at his face in a mirror and, after looking at himself, goes away and immediately forgets what he looks like. But the man who looks intently into the perfect law that gives freedom, and continues to do this, not forgetting what he has heard, but doing it—he will be blessed in what he does (James 1:23-25).

PROBLEMS IN UNDERSTANDING THE BIBLE

1. The New Testament was written almost **2,000** years ago, and the Old Testament is even older. This naturally leads to some problems in our understanding of the text.

2. Differences in culture:
   - we've never had a **king**;

   - we've (probably) never farmed or raised **sheep**;

   - we've never performed an Old Testament **sacrifice**;

   - we don't live in **tribes**;

   - we've never lived under the oppression of the **Philistines**;

   - we've never lived in a house made of mud, straw, and **brick**;

   - we don't live in a Hellenistic **culture**;

   - we don't have a formal **priesthood**;

   - we don't travel by camel or **donkey**;

   - we don't write on papyrus or **clay tablets**.

THREE STRIKES:
If someone told you they always strike out when they take a test, then you know that they are terrible test takers. Would you know what they mean if you never heard about the game of baseball?

3. Differences in **language**.
(The Hebrew reads right to left.)

4. Differences in common **knowledge**. The author is writing to an audience that has a specific point of reference as to the context of what is written. The letters of the New Testament were written for a specific purpose, and we often know very little about what that was. It's like listening in on a phone conversation or reading a letter from someone you don't know to someone you've never met. When the Old Testament talks about the "Kings of Israel," it is giving an incomplete picture and reference to another book.

As for the other events of Solomon's reign—all he did and the wisdom he displayed—are they not written in the book of the annals of Solomon? (1 Kings 11:41).

5. We are filled with our own **assumptions**.

6. The key to understanding the Bible is to first understand it in its own context and then bring that truth into **today**.

FINAL THOUGHTS

Congratulations! You made it through a lot of material. If some of it was confusing, don't worry!

Most of the material in this lesson is background information, relevant to reading the Bible. Hopefully, you've learned some things that will fill in the gaps and help you understand the Bible next time you read it.

Our challenge to you: Go back to the section called "8 images the Bible uses to describe itself," read through it again, and reflect on how the Bible should impact your life. It's our prayer that your love for God's Word will grow.

APPENDIX A:
Advanced Bible Study Method

Here is a good process to use in interpreting a particular biblical text.

(Step 1) Observation: What does the author say?

(a) Read and survey a unit of Scripture (book, chapter, pericope, paragraph).

(b) Read and survey the context.

(c) Ask questions (Who? Where? When? What?).

  - Who are the characters?

  - Where is the unit occurring?

  - When is the unit occurring?

  - What is happening?

(d) Title the unit.

(e) State the theme of the unit in one sentence.

(f) Outline, diagram, and/or chart the unit.

> **PERICOPE:**
> Another word for a context-defined unit of Scripture. The parable of the Good Samaritan is a pericope.

(Step 2) What did the author originally mean?

(a) Ask questions (Who? Where? When? What?).

- Introduction	Is there an introductory sentence or paragraph?
- Interrogation	Why? How? Who? Where? When? What?
- Comparison	How are things similar?
- Contrast	How are things different?
- Interchange	Are there alternating elements?
- Unifying Theme	What theme permeates the unit?
- Continuity	How does theme relate to the context?
- Cause and Effect	Does one action or statement cause another?
- Progression	How are themes developed?
- Repetition	Are there any ideas or phrases repeated?
- Cruciality	Is the unit arranged around one pivotal point?
- Summarization	Is there a portion of the unit that summarizes the activity or thought of the unit?

(b) Study major terms.

(c) Summarize and evaluate meaning of unit as a whole.

(Step 3) Understanding and Application: What does it mean for today?

(a) Evaluate: What have you learned? What principles does the unit teach that have meaning for every age? What are the results?

(b) Meditate on the theological, spiritual, and ethical implications.

(c) Dedicate the principles you've discovered to your life:

  - What has been said to me?

  - How should my attitudes respond to these truths?

  - How should my behavior respond to these truths?

(d) Communicate:

  - What applies only to your life?

  - What would you teach to others?

  - How would you teach this to others?

SURVEY OF THE NEW TESTAMENT

ROOTED:NEW TESTAMENT

study two survey of the new testament

TABLE OF CONTENTS

content of the new testament books

QUICK HISTORY OF THE NEW TESTAMENT

[persia]

1. At the close of the Old Testament, the major world power was Persia (present-day Iran). It was under Persian rule that Israel was allowed to return home and rebuild its country about 458 B.C.

2. Persia became weak from quick expansion and bitter infighting, and soon disappeared as a world power about 324 B.C.

[greece (macedonia)]

1. Philip II united all of the independent Greek city-states and created an empire. When he died, his son, Alexander the Great became **king** about 336 B.C.

2. Alexander the Great had a massive army, and in less than 15 years, he conquered nearly all the known world. In order to control his new lands, he imposed his culture upon the conquered countries. This process was called **Hellenism**. The changes consisted mainly of language, holidays, customs, and worship of Greek gods.

3. Alexander died at a young age (33). His vast empire was divided into five parts, one for each of his generals. Only two of the empires concern us as we seek to better **understand** the New Testament.

[ptolemaic and seleucid empires]

1. The Ptolemaic Empire was south of Israel, in Egypt. The Seleucid Empire was north of Israel, in **Syria** and Babylon (what is now Iraq).

2. Both of these empires fought against each other, and often the battleground was **Israel**.

3. Both kingdoms continued Hellenism in their lands. In Israel, the Seleucids went so far as to **outlaw** Jewish practices, persecute the Jews, and desecrate the Temple.

4. The nation of Israel eventually revolted against the Seleucids and won back its **independence** (circa 168 B.C. to 37 B.C.). However, because of internal struggles, it was ripe for conquest by the up-and-coming power of Rome.

[roman empire]

1. After **defeating** several of Rome's enemies, Pompey, a Roman general, took control of Israel (also called Palestine) in 63 B.C. Not until 1948 would Israel regain its political independence.

2. Rome stopped its expansion and turned to a period of peace. This was called the Pax Romana. Rome had very few internal struggles. Civilization developed quickly through many **advancements**.

Key Note: One of the advancements was the construction of the famous "Roman roads," which connected the entire Empire. Although there were few Roman roads in Israel, they would become extremely helpful for the apostle Paul, and others, as they spread the Gospel to the world.

3. In Israel, Rome allowed native vassals, or kings, to rule. The first was Herod the Great (ruled 37 B.C. to 4 A.D.), a person from Edom. He was **ruthless** and cruel. (How cruel? He killed two of his wives and three of his sons.)

4. Life in Israel was very difficult under Roman rule. But it was at least **peaceful**. (Note: Except for the Zealots, which are mentioned later.)

[wrap-up and quick review]

After Jewish exile in Babylon:
   - The Jews return and rebuild their nation.

   - Alexander the Great takes control over Palestine (Israel).

   - Ptolemies take control over Palestine.

   - Seleucids take control over Palestine.

   - Jews revolt against the Seleucids.

   - Jews win independence.

   - Rome takes control of Palestine.

   - Jews revolt and lose.

   - Roman rule was difficult for the Israelites.

Understanding the historical background makes reading the Bible easier and more interesting. It's like turning a black and white image into full color.

THE CULTURAL AND RELIGIOUS SETTING

[hellenism]

1. The spread of Greek culture, philosophy, language, and style that began with Alexander the Great continued through the **Roman** period.

2. Alexander spread Hellenism to make his rule manageable. Imposing his Greek culture on others made it possible for him to govern such a huge **empire**. (And it later benefited the Romans when they conquered the world.)

3. Greek influence spread across the entire spectrum of human society: from "surface" areas like clothes and language to "deep" areas like **religion** and philosophy.

For many conquered people groups, Hellenism was an enlightenment compared to their own culture. The Greeks were very advanced in scholarship, art, and medicine.

For some, like the Jews, it was an imposition and a curse. Immorality was also a characteristic of Hellenism.

4. Here lies the problem for the Jews. Hellenism became a huge **dividing** factor for the once unified people who sought to follow the Old Covenant.

Some Jews accepted and desired Hellenism, others **rejected** and fought against it.

[judaism]

1. By the time of the New Testament, the Jewish faith was far **different** than 400 years prior (during the time of the prophets).

2. The exile and utter defeat of the Jewish nation (fall of Samaria and Jerusalem) took many Jews out of their **homeland**. When Jesus walked the earth, more Jews lived outside of Israel than inside.

3. Without the temple in which to worship God, the Jews had to find new ways to worship and keep their **identity** as a people. Two major developments occurred:
   (a) Learning and **studying** the Torah became the highest "calling" for a Jew.
   (b) The "Synagogue" was created and became the place to worship, instead of the Temple. For worship, animal sacrifices were replaced by **learning**.

4. Without these developments, the culture and beliefs of the Jewish people could have been lost to **history**. These changes ensured the survival of Jewish culture and identity.

[pharisees]

1. The Pharisees accepted the whole Old Testament, but also added **oral** tradition as equally authoritative. They were fairly liberal in their understanding and interpretation of Scripture.

2. Most Pharisees were either rich or financially comfortable. Their goal was to bring their interpretation of the Word of God to the **people**.

3. Pharisees did not practice a temple-focused religion (with the endless animal sacrifices). Instead, they tried to move Jewish practices into the **home**.

4. Pharisees emphasized moral and ethical codes rather than theology or a **heart** turned toward God.

5. Pharisees believed in angels and in life after **death**.

6. Pharisees viewed the Roman government as acceptable, as long as it didn't put constraints on Jewish **practices**.

[essenes]

1. The Essenes lived in extreme separation from society. They had a very low opinion of women, and therefore, married rarely. They followed a very, very strict observance of the **Sabbath**. Initiation for those wanting to join this sect took three years. They lived communally, sharing everything.

2. The Essenes rejected everyone but themselves: The Romans and the Jews were unclean and impure. They considered themselves the **true** Israel.

3. The Essenes accepted the whole Old Testament as Scripture along with some of their own writings. They had an extensive **angel** theology.

4. The Essenes are not directly mentioned in the New Testament.

[sadducees]

1. The Sadducees were made up of mostly upper-class Priests and held a significant amount of **political** power in Israel.

2. The Sadducees had a very narrow acceptance of Scripture, rejecting the moral law of the Pharisees, the prophets, and other historical or poetic writings. Only the **five books** of Moses were accepted.

3. The Sadducees had a very wide view of politics. They were mostly accepting, even **supportive**, of Roman rule.

4. The Sadducees did not believe in the active role of the Holy Spirit. They did not believe in angels or the **resurrection** of the dead.

5. The Sadducees affirmed the temple cult (Levitical purity and sacrifices), but held a **distant** view of God, believing He was disinterested in human affairs.

[zealots]

1. These people had a minimal religious agenda. They were loyal patriots to the Jewish state and **traditions**.

2. They were completely opposed to all forms of Roman (or any foreign) rule. They did not agree on paying tribute to Caesar, or using the **Greek** language.

3. Their major goal was political **independence** from Rome.
Jesus interacted with all kinds of people. The better we understand them, the better we will understand His message.

STRUCTURE OF THE NEW TESTAMENT

[gospels and acts]

1. Each of the four Gospels provide different and complementary pictures of Jesus' life, ministry, and **teaching**.

2. The book of Acts records the **history** of the early church, and the spread of the Gospel from Jerusalem to Rome.

3. The books of this division are:
   - Matthew

   - Mark

   - Luke

   - John

   - Acts

[pauline letters]

1. Nearly all of Paul's letters were written for a **specific** occasion and purpose.

2. None of the Pauline letters is a complete "textbook" for theology. They are Paul's application of theology to the **real life** situations either the church or individuals were going through.

3. The books of this division are:

- Romans

- 1 and 2 Corinthians

- Galatians

- Ephesians

- Philippians

- Colossians

- 1 and 2 Thessalonians

- 1 and 2 Timothy

- Titus

- Philemon

[general letters]

1. These letters were written by different Apostles to encourage, instruct, and guide **believers**.

2. The books of this division are:

   - Hebrews

   - James

   - 1 and 2 Peter

   - 1, 2, and 3 John

   - Jude

[revelation]

1. This book records John's visions of the **end times**.

CONTENT OF THE NEW TESTAMENT BOOKS

[matthew]

1. The author was Matthew, a tax collector Jesus called to be one of His **disciples** (see Matthew 9:9).

2. This book is clearly written for **Jewish** readers. Not only does this Gospel contain the most Old Testament quotations, but the author also uses Hebrew terms when the other Gospels use Greek equivalents. (For example, it uses "Rabbi" instead of "teacher".)

3. Matthew highlights Jesus' relationship to the Jewish faith. Jesus fulfilled every law and **prophecy** in the Old Testament. He also came to challenge the Jews for their unfaithfulness.

4. Matthew shows Jesus as the Master **Teacher**.

[mark]

1. The author of the second Gospel is John Mark, a close companion of the famous disciple, **Peter**. He was a young man when Jesus started his public ministry. His house was probably a meeting place for believers (Acts 12:12). He was likely associated with Jesus' ministry (see Mark 14:51-52).

2. This Gospel account was intended for the church in Rome (Gentile readers). Mark explains Jewish customs and seems to show an interest in **persecution** and martyrdom.

3. Mark shows Jesus as a man of **action**: Jesus is always on the go and never in one place for long. Romans understood and admired men of action.

[luke]

1. The author of the third Gospel is Luke, a **Gentile** physician who was a close associate of the Apostle Paul.

2. This book is addressed to a specific person, to "most excellent Theophilus" (Luke 1:3). Theophilus was probably a Roman official of some sort, who was most likely going to make sure Luke's works (Luke and Acts) got **distributed**. The purpose of this book is clearly stated in 1:4, *so that you may know the certainty of the things you have been taught.* (Note: Some scholars say that since Theophilus means "lover of God," that Luke could have been writing to any Gentile Christian).

3. The Gospel of Luke stresses the blessings and salvation Jesus brings to those who believe through grace. No man or woman can **earn** God's blessings.

[john]

1. The fourth Gospel was written by Jesus' **closest** disciple, John.

2. This Gospel was written much later than the other Gospels and is very **different** in content, style, and structure. Its purpose is clear:

But these are written that you may believe that Jesus is the Christ, the Son of God, and that by believing you may have life in his name (John 20:31).

3. John emphasizes the dual nature and **mystery** of Jesus: God became man.

[acts]

1. The book of Acts was also written by **Luke** and is a continuation of the third Gospel.

2. Acts records the beginnings of the spread of the early church, which started in Jerusalem and ended up in **Rome**.

3. Acts describes the ministries of Peter and then Paul. Peter was an apostle to the Jews and Paul brought the Gospel to the **Gentiles**.

4. If the Gospels are a testimony about Jesus, then Acts shows the power of the Holy Spirit. It wasn't great men like Peter and Paul (and the rest of the disciples) who spread the Gospel. It was (and still is) the **power** of the Holy Spirit.

[romans]

1. Paul wrote this letter to the church in Rome; which was very likely a Gentile congregation. This letter was a preparation for his first visit to this church.

2. Major themes in the book of Romans:
   (a) sinfulness (or imperfection) of people;

   (b) justification through faith;

   (c) sanctification of believers;

   (d) Israel's unbelief.

> **JUSTIFICATION:**
> Made right before God. Justification describes the process a non-believer undergoes when he or she becomes a believer. Believers no longer need to fear judgment from God, as they have been made right (or justified) before Him.

> **SANCTIFICATION:**
> The holy living of believers. This is a life-long process where a Christian becomes more like Christ.

3. Key verse:

I am not ashamed of the gospel, because it is the power of God for the salvation of everyone who believes: first for the Jew, then for the Gentile. For in the gospel a righteousness from God is revealed, a righteousness that is by faith from first to last, just as it is written: "The righteous will live by faith" (Romans 1:16-17).

[1 corinthians]

1. Paul wrote this letter to the church in Corinth, which he had **started** earlier in his ministry.

2. This letter is a response to a letter the Corinthians had written to Paul. Paul also addresses reports of **disunity** (along with some other problems) in the church at Corinth.

3. Most of the themes of this book deal with how a Christian is to act:

   (a) the unity of Christ and his church;

   (b) how to deal with immoral Christians;

   (c) public worship and spiritual gifts;

   (d) the importance of the resurrection.

4. Key verse:

If there is no resurrection of the dead, then not even Christ has been raised. And if Christ has not been raised, our preaching is useless and so is your faith (1 Corinthians 15:13-14).

[2 corinthians]

1. After Paul wrote 1 Corinthians, he made a short "painful visit" to the church in Corinth. His visit was unsuccessful. That is, it did not change them. So he wrote a "sorrowful letter" which was **lost** to the church when the New Testament was put together. After receiving Paul's "sorrowful letter," the Corinthians changed their hearts and their actions. When Paul heard this positive response, he wrote what we know as 2 Corinthians.

A Chronology of Paul's Relationship with the Corinthians

- 1 Corinthians written

- "Painful visit" by Paul

- "Sorrowful letter" written

- Paul hears the good news of their change

- 2 Corinthians written

2. This letter, like any **personal** letter, is especially difficult to analyze. Often it goes off into side issues. Some of the themes are:

(a) God's **comfort** in troubles;

(b) the **superiority** of the Gospel over the law;

(c) our **confidence** now because of a real future with God.

3. Key verse:

We are hard pressed on every side, but not crushed; perplexed, but not in despair; persecuted, but not abandoned; struck down, but not destroyed. We always carry around in our body the death of Jesus, so that the life of Jesus may also be revealed in our body (2 Corinthians 4:8-10).

[galatians]

1. Paul wrote this letter to a **region** of a few churches rather than a single church.
(Most of his letters were meant to be circulated to many churches.)

2. Paul wrote this letter to fight against the problem of "Judaizers." These were Jewish Christians who made Jewish **customs** (like circumcision) a requirement to be a Christian.

3. What is the problem with this? Judaizers added to the Gospel religious rituals more tied to the Jewish faith. The result being that God's free gift of salvation still had to be **earned**.

4. Major themes include:
   (a) the **authority** of the Gospel, and Paul's ministry;

   (b) freedom;

   (c) salvation is by **faith**, not "observing the law";

   (d) Christians' responsibility: **serve** one another in love.

5. Key verse:
I would like to learn just one thing from you: Did you receive the Spirit by observing the law, or by believing what you heard? Are you so foolish? After beginning with the Spirit, are you now trying to attain your goal by human effort? (Galatians 3:2-3)

[ephesians]

1. Paul's letter to the church in Ephesus was not written as a response to a specific **problem** or heresy.

2. This book emphasizes the church as Christ's body and the unity and **blessings** all believers share.

3. Some major themes include:
   (a) all Christians have been **chosen** according to God's plan;

   (b) **salvation** by grace, the unity of all believers;

   (c) Christians' responsibility: be **imitators** of God;

   (d) God's **protection** for our life (God's armor).

4. Key verse:
Put on the full armor of God so that you can take your stand against the devil's schemes (Ephesians 6:11).

[philippians]

1. Philippians is Paul's letter of joy to the church at Philippi, which was his **favorite** church. Paul wrote this letter from prison to express his joy over the spread of the Gospel in and around the Philippian church.

2. There was a possible threat of Judaizers, as chapter 3:1-6 seems to be speaking against Jewish **legalists**.

3. Major themes include:
   (a) joy and **rejoicing**, even in difficult times;

   (b) the **humility** of Christ;

   (c) the foolishness of **accomplishments** without Christ;

   (d) Christian; responsibility: working out **salvation**.

4. Key verse:
Whatever happens, conduct yourselves in a manner worthy of the gospel of Christ. Then, whether I come and see you or only hear about you in my absence, I will know that you stand firm in one spirit, contending as one man for the faith of the gospel (Philippians 1:27).

[colossians]

1. Paul's letter to the church in Colossae was written to **combat** several varied heresies (defined as: a religious belief opposed to the main doctrines of the church). Colossae had a long history and sat on major trade routes. Thus, it had many different kinds of people living there.

2. These many different people groups meant different **ideas**, religions, and philosophies. This letter was written to argue against the so-called "Colossian Heresy," which was a mix of:
   - Jewish legalism (circumcision and food regulations)

   - Early Gnosticism (beliefs combining Greek philosophy, Oriental mysticism, and Christian theology)

   - Mysticism (worship of angels)

3. Major themes include:

  (a) the supremacy of **Christ**;

  (b) Christ as the **head** of the church;

  (c) Christians are to be **focused** on Christ, not earthly things.

4. Key verse:

See to it that no one takes you captive through hollow and deceptive philosophy, which depends on human tradition and the basic principles of this world rather than on Christ (Colossians 2:8).

[1 thessalonians]

1. Thessalonica was the capital of Macedonia and boasted of **200,000** inhabitants. It was a seaport town, connecting Rome with the East.

2. Paul wasn't able to stay in Thessalonica for very long (one month), so he wrote this letter soon after he was **forced** to leave by the Thessalonian Jews.

3. Some major themes include:

  (a) faith, love, and **hope**;

  (b) **living** to please God;

  (c) the second **coming** of Jesus.

4. Key verse:

We loved you so much that we were delighted to share with you not only the gospel of God but our lives as well, because you had become so dear to us (1 Thessalonians 2:8).

[2 thessalonians]

1. This letter wasn't written too long after the first letter to the Thessalonians (perhaps six months). It contains many of the same elements, as the church's situation hadn't changed. They were being **persecuted** and they were immature in their understanding of Jesus.

2. One major misunderstanding concerned the second coming of Christ. Many in the church had stopped **working** because they thought Jesus would return soon. Because of this, much of this letter is about eschatology (end times).

3. Major themes include:
   (a) **encouragement** in suffering;

   (b) "Man of lawlessness," the **Anti-Christ**;

   (c) Warnings against not **working**.

4. Key verse:
But we ought always to thank God for you, brothers loved by the Lord, because from the beginning God chose you to be saved through the sanctifying work of the Spirit and through belief in the truth (2 Thessalonians 2:13).

[1 timothy]

1. Paul wrote this letter to his spiritual son, Timothy, in order to give him **pastoral** advice.

2. Timothy received this letter while he was pastoring in **Ephesus**.

3. Some of Paul's exhortations to Timothy include:
   (a) warnings against **false** teachers;

   (b) public worship **instructions**;

   (c) church **officials** (elders and deacons);

   (d) how **widows**, elders, and slaves are to be treated.

4. Key verse:
Don't let anyone look down on you because you are young, but set an example for the believers in speech, in life, in love, in faith and in purity (1 Timothy 4:12).

[2 timothy]

1. This letter is the last Paul ever wrote. He was at the end of his life, in a Roman prison, waiting to be executed because of his **faith**.

2. Major exhortations to Timothy:
   (a) do not be **ashamed**, but be strong in the Lord;

   (b) foolish **speech**: quarreling, godless chatter, stupid arguments;

   (c) godlessness will come in the **last** days.

3. Key verse:
All Scripture is God-breathed and is useful for teaching, rebuking, correcting and training in righteousness, so that the man of God may be thoroughly equipped for every good work (2 Timothy 3:16-17).

[titus]

1. Titus was a Gentile pastor whom Paul had left on the island of Crete. The Cretans' dishonesty, **gluttony**, and laziness were legendary, but Titus was an able co-worker of Paul.

2. Some of Paul's exhortations to Titus were:
   (a) watch out for **false** teachers;

   (b) qualifications of church **leaders**;

   (c) what to **teach** to different groups.

3. Key verse:
But when the kindness and love of God our Savior appeared, he saved us, not because of righteous things we had done, but because of his mercy (Titus 3:4-5).

[philemon]

1. Paul wrote this short letter (only 25 verses!) to Philemon, owner of the slave, Onesimus. Onesimus had **stolen** many things from Philemon, and had then run away from him—a crime punishable by death.

2. Philemon was a "dear friend and fellow worker" of Paul, thus Paul thought he could **plead** for Onesimus on his behalf.

3. Key verse:
So if you consider me a partner, welcome him as you would welcome me. If he has done you any wrong or owes you anything, charge it to me (Philemon 17-18).

[hebrews]

1. The early church fathers thought this book was written by Paul, but they weren't 100 percent certain (which is why it is placed after Philemon). Modern scholars have **proven** otherwise.

2. Although its authorship is not certain (some think Apollos from Acts 18:24 could have been the author), this does not take away from the book's powerful message. Thoroughly Jewish in character, this letter is pivotal in understanding the Old Testament in light of **Christ**.

3. Major themes of this book include:
   (a) Christ's superiority over **angels**, Moses, and the Levitical priesthood;

   (b) Christ as the **perfect** High Priest;

   (c) great people of **faith**;

   (d) Christians' responsibility: **love** each other, praise God.

4. Key verse:
For we do not have a high priest who is unable to sympathize with our weaknesses, but we have one who has been tempted in every way, just as we are—yet was without sin. Let us then approach the throne of grace with confidence, so that we may receive mercy and find grace to help us in our time of need (Hebrews 4:15-16).

[james]

1. James was written by Jesus' brother, James, the **leader** of the Jerusalem church.

2. James is purely practical. Its theology drives straight to the point of Christian living: Faith without **works** is no faith at all.

3. Some of the major themes in James are:
   (a) persevering through **trials**;

   (b) not showing **favoritism**;

   (c) taming your **tongue**;

   (d) watching out for **worldliness**.

4. Key verse:
In the same way, faith by itself, if it is not accompanied by action, is dead (James 2:17).

[1 peter]

1. This letter was written by the apostle Peter, written to "God's elect . . . scattered throughout [the world]." Persecution from the Romans was just beginning and 1 Peter is a letter to **comfort** believers.

2. Some of the major themes include:
   (a) faith (in Christ) and **hope** (of His return);

   (b) holy **living**;

   (c) submission to **political** authority;

   (d) suffering for doing **good**.

3. Key verse:

. . . who through faith are shielded by God's power until the coming of the salvation that is ready to be revealed in the last time (1 Peter 1:5).

[2 peter]

1. Peter's first letter was a comfort from persecution outside the Church. This letter is a warning against **false** teachers, "evil doers," and dangers from within the Church.

2. The purposes and themes of this letter are:

   (a) to stimulate Christian **growth**;

   (b) to combat **false** teaching;

   (c) to **encourage** watchfulness of Christ's return.

3. Key verse:

The Lord is not slow in keeping his promise, as some understand slowness. He is patient with you, not wanting anyone to perish, but everyone to come to repentance (2 Peter 3:9).

[1 john]

1. The writer of this letter is the disciple "whom Jesus loved," John, author of the fourth Gospel and Revelation. This letter was written to believers in general, to argue strongly against an **early form** of Gnosticism.

2. The two central teachings to Gnosticism were:

   (a) matter (physical) is **evil**, and spirit is good;

   (b) salvation is through secret **knowledge**.

3. The central purposes of 1 John were to:

   (a) expose false **teachers**;

   (b) give **assurance** of salvation.

4. Key verse:

I write these things to you who believe in the name of the Son of God so that you may know that you have eternal life (1 John 5:13).

[2 john and 3 john]

1. Similar to 1 John, these letters were written to expose false teachers and **encourage** believers.

2. These letters teach that true love is **obedience** to Christ's commands.

3. Key verses:

Anyone who runs ahead and does not continue in the teaching of Christ does not have God; whoever continues in the teaching has both the Father and the Son (2 John 9).

Dear friend, do not imitate what is evil but what is good. Anyone who does what is good is from God. Anyone who does what is evil has not seen God (3 John 11).

[jude]

1. The author of Jude was **Judas**, the brother of Jesus and James.
Note: This is not the Judas who betrayed Jesus.

2. This letter defends the **grace** of God: rely on Jesus; do not deny him.

3. Key verse:

But you, dear friends, build yourselves up in your most holy faith and pray in the Holy Spirit (Jude 20).

[revelation]

1. This well-known, and often misinterpreted letter, was written by John. It was the last book written of the New Testament, a time when worship of the Roman **emperor** was being forced upon Christians.

2. Purpose: to encourage Christians to remain **faithful** to God. Its message, in short, is that God is in control of history and He wins in the end.

3. Key verses:

Blessed is the one who reads the words of this prophecy, and blessed are those who hear it and take to heart what is written in it, because the time is near (Revelation 1:3).

Then I saw a new heaven and a new earth, for the first heaven and the first earth had passed away, and there was no longer any sea. I saw the Holy City, the new Jerusalem, coming down out of heaven from God, prepared as a bride beautifully dressed for her husband (Revelation 21:1-2).

[so what do i do now?]
The purpose of this lesson was to give you an overview of the New Testament so you can better understand it when you read it. Now that you've had a quick look at each book in the New Testament, choose one this week to begin studying.

Share this with a leader so he/she can hold you accountable.

THE LIFE AND TEACHINGS OF JESUS

ROOTED:NEW TESTAMENT

ROOTED: NEW TESTAMENT

study three the life and teachings of Jesus

TABLE OF CONTENTS

PART I: THE LIFE OF JESUS

MEANING AND IMPACT

[Jesus' life]

The life Jesus lived is the supreme example of **perfection**. Our response should be **obedience**—to follow His example as best we can with the Holy Spirit's help and power.

[Jesus' death]

When Jesus died on the cross, He paid our **debt** to God. Our response should be in **faith**. We need to accept that Jesus paid the penalty for our sin (John 1:12).

But God demonstrates his own love for us in this: While we were still sinners, Christ died for us (Romans 5:8).

[the secret]

1. It is a **vast** understatement to say that Jesus' life had tremendous meaning and **impact** on the world. What was His secret?

2. In everything that Jesus did, He lived in **obedience** to God.
Jesus gave them this answer: "I tell you the truth, the Son can do nothing by himself; he can do only what he sees his Father doing, because whatever the Father does the Son also does" (John 5:19).

MAJOR DETAILS

[birth of Jesus]

1. The beginnings of the most effective life on earth were both **humble** and **miraculous**.

2. Jesus was conceived by the **Holy Spirit** and His mother, Mary, was a **virgin**. He was born in a cave that was used as a stable.

3. Although the virgin birth was a miracle, the real miracle was the **incarnation**, which means **God** became **man**.

[john the baptist]

Before Jesus began His ministry, there was a man named John the Baptist who **prepared** the people for Jesus with his preaching and call to **spiritual** renewal. It was prophesied that he would appear before the coming of the Messiah in several Old Testament passages.

[learning in the temple]

1. When Jesus was a boy, He "sat" among the **teachers**, listening to them and asking them questions.

2. When God became a person, He **limited** His own powers (e.g., Jesus couldn't be in two places at once).

[baptism by john]

1. To symbolize a new **commitment** to serving God, John the Baptist baptized many people. Jesus went to John to be baptized, although John didn't want to baptize the Son of God.

2. After Jesus was baptized, the **sky** opened up, the Holy Spirit descended upon Jesus, and God the Father spoke: *And a voice from Heaven said, "This is my Son, whom I love; with him I am well pleased" (Matthew 3:17).*

[temptation in the desert]

1. Soon after His baptism, Jesus went into the **desert** because He was **led** by the Holy Spirit.

2. After **fasting** (not eating) for 40 days, the devil came to Jesus to tempt Him with food, tried to cause Jesus to **doubt** God's power, and offered Jesus "all the Kingdoms of the earth."

3. Jesus fought each of the devil's three temptations with **Scripture**.

[beginning of His public ministry]

1. Jesus went to Nazareth, His **hometown**. On the Sabbath He went to the synagogue (Jewish place of worship).

2. The normal service included a person reading the day's **selection** of Scripture. Jesus read a portion of **Isaiah**; it was a prophecy about the coming Messiah. After reading it, Jesus said He was the Messiah, and the people became angry.

[calling of the disciples]

1. Jesus attracted many **followers**, but He had **12** who were special and were with Him nearly all of the time. (Discussion Question: What are the obvious and not-so-obvious differences of following Jesus today versus 2,000 years ago?)

2. Although all of the disciples were Jewish, many of them were very **different** from one another. All of them gave up their old **lives** to follow Jesus.

[sermons, parables, and miracles]

1. Jesus spent much of His ministry preaching **sermons** to small groups, as well as crowds as large as 5,000 men (this number could have been quadrupled if you added women and children). His favorite tool in sermons was the **parable**. (Something we will talk about later.)

2. Jesus also performed many awesome **miracles** for people in need. Jesus' life and ministry never became too busy for individuals: the Gospels record several **significant** one-on-one conversations and interactions.
Jesus did many other things as well. If every one of them were written down, I suppose that even the whole world would not have room for the books that would be written (John 21:25).

[transfiguration]

1. In this event, Jesus took His three closest disciples up to a mountain to **pray**. While they were praying, Jesus was "transfigured." Matthew says, "his face shone like the sun and his clothes became **white** as light" (Matthew 17:2).

2. This unbelievable event was a **sneak preview** of the glory to come in Heaven. This also was another supernatural event demonstrating the deity of Christ and His authority from God. (Deity: the state of being God; divine nature; godhood.)

[last supper]

1. The last night Jesus had with His friends (12 disciples) was spent celebrating the **Passover** (a Jewish holiday which was a reminder of the exodus from Egypt).

2. The Passover was a celebration of God's **redemption** of the Jewish nation from the bondage they faced in Egypt. Jesus redefined the holiday through two symbols: bread and wine. These two elements are reminders to Christians of Jesus' broken body (bread) and spilled blood (wine). His sacrifice that **redeemed** us from our bondage to sin.

3. At the Last Supper, Jesus also **predicted** who would betray Him—Judas.

[garden of gethsemane]

1. Retreating to a quiet **garden** for prayer, Jesus was alone with the awesome and difficult task set before Him.

2. His stress was so great it caused His **sweat** to fall like "drops of blood."

3. Although a part of Jesus didn't want to die on the Cross, He did it anyway because it was God's **will**.

4. It was here, in the garden, where Jesus was **betrayed** by Judas and arrested by the Jews.

[trial of Jesus]

1. After His arrest, Jesus was **accused** by the Jews of being a blasphemer (a person who lies about God). Jesus claimed to be God and the Jews thought that was a lie. The Jews couldn't **punish** Jesus, however, because they were under the authority of Roman law.

2. The Jews then handed Jesus over to the **Romans** for judgment. The Jews told the Romans, "Jesus claims to be a **King**." The Romans didn't like other kings because they wanted to remain in power with their own king (called Caesar).

3. The Romans **questioned** Jesus, but He remained silent. They found nothing wrong with Him, but the Jews worked a mob who wanted Jesus' death up into a **frenzy**. Wanting to avoid a riot, the Romans sentenced Jesus to die.

4. Jesus was asked dozens of questions by the Jewish elders and by two different Roman officials, but He remained silent before all of their questions except two. Jesus said He was born to be a **King**, and that He was the Son of God.

[death and resurrection]

1. After being beaten horribly, Jesus was forced to carry very heavy wooden beams. Jesus was sentenced to die by crucifixion, a **common** Roman death sentence. Dying on a cross was extremely painful because it slowly **suffocated** the condemned as he had to push up on the nail to catch a breath. (Imagine a deep sliver. Now imagine a nail through both feet with all of your weight resting on it for nine hours).

2. Even in the midst of His terrible pain and suffering, Jesus' ministry did not **stop**. Not only did He make an impact on a dying criminal, but He also **prayed** for the people who tortured Him and put Him to death.

3. After Jesus died, He was buried in a tomb that was a small cave with a huge rock rolled in front. The Jews knew Jesus said He would rise from the dead and they were afraid that the disciples would **steal** the body. A group of **guards** were deployed to watch the tomb to make it as secure as they could.

4. Jesus died on a Friday and rose from the dead on Sunday morning. The first people to find out Jesus was no longer dead were **women**. After a conversation with an angel, the women quickly ran and told the **disciples**.

[appearances]

After His resurrection, Jesus was on the earth for about a **month**. During this time He appeared to many people, offering encouragement and final **instructions**.

For what I received I passed on to you as of first importance: that Christ died for our sins according to the Scriptures, that he was buried, that he was raised on the third day according to the Scriptures, and that he appeared to Peter, and then to the Twelve. After that, he appeared to more than five hundred of the brothers at the same time, most of whom are still living, though some have fallen asleep. Then he appeared to James, then to all the apostles, and last of all he appeared to me also, as to one abnormally born (1 Corinthians 15:3-8).

[ascension into Heaven]

On one occasion, while he [Jesus] was eating with them, he gave them this command: "Do not leave Jerusalem, but wait for the gift my Father promised, which you have heard me speak about. For John baptized with water, but in a few days you will be baptized with the Holy Spirit." So when they met together, they asked him, "Lord, are you at this time going to restore the kingdom to Israel?" He said to them: "It is not for you to know the times or dates the Father has set by his own authority. But you will receive power when the Holy Spirit comes on you; and you will be my witnesses in Jerusalem, and in all Judea and Samaria, and to the ends of the earth." After he said this, he was taken up before their very eyes, and a cloud hid him from their sight (Acts 1:4-9).

MIRACLES

[snapshots of the supernatural]

1. Miracles are **acts** of God that deviate from our understanding of the laws of **nature**.

2. Because God created and **sustains** nature and its laws, miracles are possible for God. Denying the existence of miracles **limits** the power of God.

3. Jesus used miracles to **increase** or create the faith of other people. Miracles were the **proof** that Jesus was from God. They are snapshots of the supernatural allowing us to see God's glory.

4. All of the miracles Jesus did can be broken down into two basic categories: **nature** miracles and **healing** miracles.

[nature miracles]

The following is the list of nature miracles Jesus did:

- water into wine	John 2:1-11
- feeding of the 5,000	Matthew 14:15-21; Mark 6:35-44; Luke 9:12-17; John 6:5-15
- stilling a storm	Matthew 8:23-27; Mark 4:35-41; Luke 8:22-25
- walking on water	Matthew 14:22-33; Mark 6:45-52
- tax money from a fish	Matthew 17:24-27
- feeding of the 4,000	Matthew 15:32-39; Mark 8:1-9
- withering of the fig tree	Matthew 21:17-22; Mark 11:12-14, 20-25
- big catch of fish	Luke 5:1-11
- another big catch of fish	John 21:1-14

[healing miracles]

The following is the list of healing miracles Jesus did:

- nobleman's son	John 4:46-54
- blind man	Mark 8:22-26
- another blind man	John 9:1-41
- raised Lazarus from the dead	John 11:1-45
- cast out demons	Matthew 8:28-33; Mark 5:1-20; Luke 8:26-39
- raised Jairus' daughter from the dead	Matthew 9:18-26; Mark 5:35-43; Luke 8:49-56

- invalid	John 5:1-13
- bleeding woman	Matthew 9:20-22; Mark 5:25-34; Luke 8:43-48
- paralytic	Matthew 9:1-8; Mark 2:1-12; Luke 5:17-26
- leper	Matthew 8:1-4; Mark 1:40-45; Luke 5:12-15
- Peter's mother-in-law	Matthew 8:14-17; Mark 1:29-31; Luke 4:38-39
- withered hand	Matthew 12:9-14; Mark 3:1-6; Luke 6:6-11
- demon-possessed child	Matthew 17:14-20; Mark 9:14-29; Luke 9:37-43
- cast out another demon	Matthew 12:22; Luke 11:14
- 2 blind men	Matthew 9:27-31, Matthew 20:29-34
- cast out another demon	Matthew 9:32-34
- deaf-mute	Mark 7:31-37
- blind man	Mark 10:46-52; Luke 18:35-42
- sick Syro-Phoenician girl	Matthew 15:21-28; Mark 7:24-30
- centurion's servant	Matthew 8:5-13; Luke 7:1-10
- cast out another demon	Mark 1:23-27; Luke 4:33-36
- raised widow's son from the dead	Luke 7:11-16
- crippled woman	Luke 13:10-13
- man with dropsy	Luke 14:1-6
- 10 men with leprosy	Luke 17:11-19
- man with his ear cut off	Luke 22:49-51; John 18:10-11

PROPHECY

[what is prophecy?]

1. Prophecy, in its broadest meaning, is God's Word communicated to people.

   (a) Prophecy can tell us about the **past** (Ezekiel 36:3).

   (b) Prophecy can tell us how to live in the **present** (1 Corinthians 14:3-4; Revelation 1:3).

   (c) Prophecy can tell us what will happen in the **future** (Joel 2:28).

2. The word "prophecy" is often used in the **narrow** sense of predicting the future.

3. Jesus fulfilled over **300** different prophecies written in the Old Testament.

[the importance of the dead sea scrolls]

1. The Dead Sea Scrolls are ancient **Hebrew** documents that contain large portions of the Old Testament.

2. The Dead Sea Scrolls date back **250** years before Jesus. The Scrolls contain hundreds of prophecies about Jesus. Other than the Dead Sea Scrolls, the oldest Old Testament evidence we have was written two centuries after Jesus. Aside from the Dead Sea Scrolls, the oldest complete Hebrew Old Testament was written **10** centuries after Jesus.

Dead Sea Scrolls	Jesus	Evidence of Hebrew O.T.	Complete Hebrew O.T.
250 B.C.		3rd Century A.D.	11th Century A.D.

3. A prophecy isn't very **authoritative** if it was written after the events which it was predicting.

[major prophecies about Jesus]

- born of a virgin	Isaiah 7:14	Matthew 1:21
- descendent of Abraham	Genesis 12:1-3; 22:18	Matthew 1:1; Galatians 3:16
- tribe of Judah	Genesis 49:10	Luke 3:23,33
- descendent of David	2 Samuel 7:12	Matthew 1:1
- born in Bethlehem	Micah 5:2	Matthew 2:1; Luke 2:4-7
- Herod's killing of infants	Jeremiah 31:15	Matthew 2:16-18
- anointed by the Holy Spirit	Isaiah 11:2	Matthew 3:16
- John preparing the way	Isaiah 40:3; Malachi 3:1	Matthew 3:1-3
- perform miracles	Isaiah 35:5	Matthew 9:35
- enter Jerusalem as a king on a donkey	Zechariah 9:9	Matthew 21:4-9
- betrayed by a friend	Psalm 41:9	Luke 22:3-6
- sold for 30 pieces of silver	Zechariah 11:12	Matthew 26:14-16
- silent before accusers	Isaiah 53:7	Matthew 27:12-19
- being mocked	Psalm 22:7	Matthew 27:31
- beaten	Isaiah 52:14	Matthew 27:26
- spit upon	Isaiah 50:6	Matthew 27:30
- pierced hands and feet	Psalm 22:16	John 20:25-29
- crucified with thieves	Isaiah 53:12	Matthew 27:38
- pierced in the side	Zechariah 12:10	John 19:34
- given gall and vinegar to drink	Psalm 69:21	Matthew 27:34
- no broken bones	Psalm 34:20	John 19:32-36
- would rise from the dead	Psalm 16:10	Mark 16:6

PART II: THE TEACHINGS OF JESUS

MAKING THE IMPACT: HIS LIFESTYLE, SERMONS, AND PARABLES

[lifestyle]

1. Jesus' **public** ministry lasted three years, and He probably died around the age of 33. Before He began His ministry, Jesus lived a godly life for 30 years—He didn't wait!

2. Jesus **modeled** prayer and going to the synagogue to worship. He didn't just do it sometimes, it was His custom. *Jesus went out as usual to the Mount of Olives, and his disciples followed him (Luke 22:39).*

He went to Nazareth, where he had been brought up, and on the Sabbath day he went into the synagogue, as was his custom. And he stood up to read (Luke 4:16).

3. Jesus also taught large crowds with magnificent sermons.

[sermons]

1. The Gospels record several sermons Jesus gave to (often) large crowds. Here are a few characteristics of His teaching:
   (a) He **adapted** His message to His audience.

   (b) He was **authoritative**.

   (c) He caused people to **think** for themselves.

   (d) He **lived** what He taught.

   (e) He was intimate with, and loved, His core of **"students"**.

   (f) He often began messages because of a casual **event**.

   (g) His favorite teaching tool was the **parable**.

[parables]

1. Parable comes from a combination of words that literally mean "to throw alongside."

2. A Parable is a historical story that is thrown alongside a truth to teach it. Usually these stories described situations that were very familiar to the original readers or listeners.

3. Parables are different from allegories in that every detail in the story doesn't necessarily have hidden meaning.

4. Why did Jesus use Parables?

   (a) Parables are easy to remember.

   (b) To communicate truth to believers, but hide it from people with hard hearts.

   He replied, "The knowledge of the secrets of the kingdom of heaven has been given to you [the disciples], but not to them [the hard of heart]" (Matthew 13:11).

THE KINGDOM OF GOD

We'll spend the rest of our time together exploring many of Jesus' central teachings.

[the definition of the kingdom of God]

1. The term "Kingdom of God" **captures** all that Jesus was about: His identity, His **ministry**, and His teaching.

2. The Kingdom of God is **everything** that is under God's rule and has God's **presence**.

[the domain of the kingdom of God]

1. Rule of God in the heart . . .
   (a) is moral (attitudes and actions), not **legal** (actions only);

   (b) is spiritual, not **physical**;

   (c) actually exists, not a **dream**.

2. Rule of God in the world . . .
   (a) community, not **individuals** only;

   (b) for every person, not a **select** few;

   (c) exists now, yet is not **fully** here.

[the duration of the kingdom of God]

1. The kingdom is here now because it came with **Jesus**, and currently exists within every **believer**.

2. The kingdom is not yet **fully** here because there are people without the kingdom, and Jesus has not yet **returned**.

3. The kingdom of God that is here now is an anticipation and **guarantee** of the kingdom to come.

THE FOUR ELEMENTS OF JESUS' TEACHING

[the nature and purpose of these "elements"]

1. These elements aren't hard and fast **categories**; nor are they the **only** way to summarize what Jesus taught.

2. The **purpose** of these elements is to provide a broad **framework** for understanding what Jesus taught. Everything Jesus taught leans toward one of the following elements.

[the biographical]

1. In this element, Jesus teaches us about **who** He was and what His ministry was about.

2. Put simply, Jesus taught that He was the Son of God, the promised Messiah who had the **authority** to forgive sins, heal the sick, and raise the dead.

3. Jesus' ministry on earth was to teach God's commandments, **serve** people, and die on the Cross for our sins.

4. Jesus came to restore the broken relationship between people and God. Everything in the biographical element of Jesus' teaching **points** to this.

Examples of the biographical element:
Jesus said to them, "My Father is always at his work to this very day, and I, too, am working" (John 5:17).

Then Jesus declared, "I am the bread of life. He who comes to me will never go hungry, and he who believes in me will never be thirsty" (John 6:35).

"We are going up to Jerusalem," he said, "and the Son of Man will be betrayed to the chief priests and teachers of the law. They will condemn him to death and will hand him over to the Gentiles, who will mock him and spit on him, flog him and kill him. Three days later he will rise" (Mark 10:33-34).

[the kingdom of God: "membership"]

1. In this element, Jesus teaches us the **boundaries** of the kingdom of God. This element defines who is of the kingdom and who is not (what it takes to be a "member").

2. There are three features to the element of kingdom membership:
   (a) entrance into the kingdom is by **faith** in Jesus;

   (b) all **people** are called to faith and the kingdom;

   (c) the "**scatter** or **gather**" principle: everyone is either in the kingdom or out of the kingdom; there is no middle ground.

Examples of the membership element:

"For God so loved the world that he gave his one and only Son, that whoever believes in him shall not perish but have eternal life" (John 3:16).

"He who is not with me is against me, and he who does not gather with me scatters" (Matthew 12:30).

"For whoever is not against us is for us" (Mark 9:40).

Jesus and his disciples went on to the villages around Caesarea Philippi. On the way he asked them, "Who do people say I am?" (Mark 8:27).

[the kingdom of God: living in the kingdom today]

1. Jesus didn't just tell people how to enter the kingdom, He also gave practical instructions for living in the kingdom here on earth, right now. This element is perhaps the largest category in the teachings of Jesus. It contains **instructions** for living life, and commands Christians to **obey** if they want to follow Christ.

2. This element is very broad as Jesus' teaching covers all **aspects** of living—external actions and internal thoughts/attitudes.

3. This element of Jesus' message is best summarized by: love **God** and love others. Everything else Jesus taught was an extension of these two commands.

Examples of living in the kingdom today:

"You are the salt of the earth. But if the salt loses its saltiness, how can it be made salty again? It is no longer good for anything, except to be thrown out and trampled by men" (Matthew 5:13).

"The most important one," answered Jesus, "is this: `Hear, O Israel, the Lord our God, the Lord is one. Love the Lord your God with all your heart and with all your soul and with all your mind and with all your strength.' The second is this: `Love your neighbor as yourself.' There is no commandment greater than these" (Mark 12:29-31).

[the kingdom of God: the promises of the future]

1. In this element, Jesus teaches about the things to **come** in the **future**—that is, our hope about eternal life.

2. Jesus' teaching about the future **does not** make up a large portion of His message. While "small" when one considers the number of verses devoted to the things to come, this element is "large" in its importance and significance for the Christian life.

3. Although the exact **sequence** of end times events aren't given to us, there are a few certainties that highlight this element:

    (a) There will be an end of time after Christ returns when everyone will be **judged**.

    (b) Among those judged will be **Satan**, and God will defeat him forever.

    (c) All Christians will spend **eternity** with God in Heaven.

Examples of the promises of the future:

Jesus said to them: "Watch out that no one deceives you. Many will come in my name, claiming, `I am he,' and will deceive many. When you hear of wars and rumors of wars, do not be alarmed. Such things must happen, but the end is still to come. Nation will rise against nation, and kingdom against kingdom. There will be earthquakes in various places, and famines. These are the beginning of birth pains" (Mark 13:5-8).

"At that time the sign of the Son of Man will appear in the sky, and all the nations of the earth will mourn. They will see the Son of Man coming on the clouds of the sky, with power and great glory. And He will send his angels with a loud trumpet call, and they will gather his elect from the four winds, from one end of the heavens to the other" (Matthew 24:30-31).

"Then the King will say to those on his right, `Come, you who are blessed by my Father; take your inheritance, the kingdom prepared for you since the creation of the world'" (Matthew 25:34).

THE SIGNIFICANCE OF JESUS' TEACHING

[faith, love, and hope]

1. Aside from His biographical teaching (His identity, His ministry), Jesus' message can be boiled down to **faith**, **love**, and **hope.**

2. Faith. Just as a newborn baby begins life breathing air, so does a Christian begin his or her life in the kingdom of God **"breathing"** faith. Faith in Jesus is something the healthy, maturing Christian should never be without.

3. Love. Jesus was an expert lover of God and lover of people. Our **attitudes** and actions today should never communicate anything other than love.

4. Hope. From our human perspective, life can be long and very difficult. Without hope in the future, the present becomes **meaningless**. Jesus knew this, and that is why He has assured us of our place in Heaven.

[so what now?]

Now that you've gone in depth and studied the life of Jesus, begin building some of the teachings you've learned into your life.

THE ACTS OF THE APOSTLES

ROOTED:NEW TESTAMENT

ROOTED:NEW TESTAMENT

study four the acts of the apostles

TABLE OF CONTENTS

THE ACTS OF THE APOSTLES

1. Although this book is called the Acts of Apostles, it focuses mostly on the ministries of Peter and Paul.

2. Acts is really part two of a two-volume work. The first volume is the Gospel of Luke.
Originally both were read **together**. Eventually part one (Luke) was associated and circulated with the other **Gospels**.

3. Acts is very unique from a historical perspective: it is our only document with information about the **early church**. Without it, we would know virtually nothing about how the Church began.

4. Acts is the perfect bridge between the Gospels and the letters.
For the Gospels: Acts is a sequel, answering the question, "So what happened to the disciples?"
For the letters: Acts is historical background, answering the question, "So who is this Paul the apostle, and what did he do?"

5. Jesus taught that God wanted a relationship with **everyone**, not just a select group. Jesus told His followers to make disciples of all men.

Acts is the testimony of how faithful Christians, through the power and direction of the Holy Spirit, worked hard to bring the Word of God to the ends of the earth (Acts 1:8).

HISTORICAL BACKGROUND

[the roman empire]

1. Rome controlled most of the **Western** world, and this created an extended period of peace.

2. Because of the famous Roman **roads**, travel by land was the best it had ever been in the history of civilization.

3. Travel by **sea** was also good, because Rome controlled all of the major seaports on the Mediterranean Sea.

4. Most people within the Roman Empire could speak some form of **Greek**.

5. Peace, good travel, and a common language aided the work of Christian **missionaries**.

[rome and christianity]

1. From Rome's perspective, Christianity was:
   (a) founded by a convicted criminal who was put to death;

   (b) rejected by the Jews as heresy;

   (c) a cause of conflict in the cities where it spread.

2. Rome's question: Was Christianity a Jewish sect or a **new religion**?

If it was a Jewish sect, then Christianity was okay, and the Jews weren't being fair to faithful Jewish followers. If it was a new religion, then Christianity could not be trusted, and should possibly be outlawed. Rome's final answer: new religion.

3. Acts enters this **debate** before the conclusion was reached.
Luke **argued** that Christianity was not a new religion, but a true continuation of the Jewish faith.

AUTHORSHIP

[was luke the author?]

1. Nearly all scholars agree that Luke, a **doctor** and companion of Paul, was the author of both the third Gospel and Acts.

2. Yet nowhere in either book does Luke **name** himself as the author.

[how do we know luke was the author?]

1. Acts 16:6-10
Paul and his companions traveled throughout the region of Phrygia and Galatia, having been kept by the Holy Spirit from preaching the word in the province of Asia. When they came to the border of Mysia, they tried to enter Bithynia, but the Spirit of Jesus would not allow them to. So they passed by Mysia and went down to Troas. During the night Paul had a vision of a man of Macedonia standing and begging him, "Come over to Macedonia and help us." After Paul had seen the vision, we got ready at once to leave for Macedonia, concluding that God had called us to preach the Gospel to them.

2. At this stage of Paul's journey, it is clear that the author of Acts joins Paul, and becomes one of his **traveling** partners.

3. In his own **letters**, Paul mentions Luke as his traveling companion (see Colossians 4:14; Philemon 24; 2 Timothy 4:11).

4. Even without the conclusive internal evidence, **tradition** and the early church fathers all agree that Luke was the author.

STRUCTURE

After its introduction, the book of Acts easily breaks itself into two major sections. Both sections contain three **subsections** that are defined by a concluding summary statement.

[introduction (1:1 to 2:41)]

Introduction: "The **Birth** of the Church"
Those who accepted his message were baptized, and about three thousand were added to their number that day (Acts 2:41).

[section 1 (2:42 to 12:24) "the gospel in the jewish world"]

Sub-section 1 (2:42 to 6:7)

"The **Early** Days in Jerusalem"

So the word of God spread. The number of disciples in Jerusalem increased rapidly, and a large number of priests became obedient to the faith (Acts 6:7).

Sub-section 2 (6:8 to 9:31)

"Critical **Events** in the Lives of Stephen, Philip, and Saul"

Then the Church throughout Judea, Galilee and Samaria enjoyed a time of peace. It was strengthened; and encouraged by the Holy Spirit, it grew in numbers, living in the fear of the Lord (Acts 9:31).

Sub-section 3 (9:32 to 12:24)

"The Gospel **Spreads** to Include all of Israel"

But the word of God continued to increase and spread (Acts 12:24).

[section 2 (12:25 to 28:31) "the gospel in the gentile world"]

Sub-section 4 (12:25 to 16:5)

"The First Missionary Journey and the Jerusalem **Council**"

So the churches were strengthened in the faith and grew daily in numbers (Acts 16:5).

Sub-section 5 (16:6 to 19:20)

"The Second and Third **Missionary** Journeys"

In this way the word of the Lord spread widely and grew in power (Acts 19:20).

Sub-section 6 (19:21 to 28:31)

"From Jerusalem to **Rome**"

Boldly and without hindrance he preached the kingdom of God and taught about the Lord Jesus Christ (Acts 28:31).

Another way to divide the book of Acts is based upon Acts 1:8. This verse traces the growth and **spread** of the Gospel.

But you will receive power when the Holy Spirit comes on you; and you will be my witnesses in Jerusalem, and in all Judea and Samaria, and to the ends of the earth (Acts 1:8).

1. In Jerusalem (Ch. 1-7)

2. In all Judea and Samaria (Ch. 8-9)

3. To the ends of the earth (Ch. 10-28)

PURPOSE OF ACTS: WHY DID LUKE WRITE ACTS?

There are at least three reasons why Luke wrote his two-volume work.

[I. proclaiming purpose]

Acts was addressed to one person, but was probably intended to be **circulated** throughout many churches. This was a common practice with written documents.

Acts was written to demonstrate the **relevance** of the Gospel.
  (a) The Gospel is a continuation of the **salvation** history begun in the Old Testament.

  (b) The Gospel is historical, and is rooted in the context of world history.

  (c) The Gospel means **universal** salvation.

  (d) The Gospel is free from observance of Jewish **law**.

  (e) The Gospel **spread** rapidly through the power and direction of the Holy Spirit.

[II. political purpose]

Acts was written to demonstrate how Christianity was not a **political threat** to Rome.
Jews were angry with Christianity and told Rome it was an illegal faith because it had a **king**.
The book of Acts, while never denying the kingship of Jesus, clearly argued the **political** harmlessness of Christianity.

[III. partnership purpose]

Acts was written to demonstrate how both Peter and Paul were on the same "**team**."

Peter: Apostle to **Jews**

Paul: Apostle to **Gentiles**

WALK-THROUGH OF THE BOOK OF ACTS

[chapter 1]

1. Luke opens with a **summary** statement of his first volume, where he wrote about "all that Jesus began to do and teach."

2. Jesus gives some final **instructions** to His disciples, telling them to wait in Jerusalem for a gift. Jesus is then taken up into Heaven.

3. The disciples choose another disciple to replace **Judas**.

[chapter 2]

1. The birth of the Church; the disciples are baptized by the Holy Spirit, and "**tongues** of fire" appear over each disciple.

2. The disciples begin to **preach** to a large crowd in different languages through the power of the Holy Spirit.

3. Peter gives his first **sermon** (the Gospel message, with Old Testament prophecy).

4. The Church forms a new **community**, where "all the believers were together and had everything in common."

[chapter 3]

1. Peter heals a **beggar**, which leads to his second sermon (healing is by God's power, the Gospel message).

2. Notice this pattern:

   Peter is going about his normal life.

   Peter offers to the beggar "what he has."

   Other people notice something different about Peter.

   Peter is ready with a **response**: Gospel message.

3. Discussion Question: How can this type of example play out in your life?

[chapter 4]

1. By now, the **religious** authorities are noticing Peter and the disciples.

2. The Sanhedrin **questions** Peter and John, and then warns them not to talk about Jesus.

3. The Church **prays** during this persecution, and believers continue to share all of their possessions.

[chapter 5]

1. Two people, Ananias and Sapphira, **lie** to the Holy Spirit. The apostles heal more people.

2. The apostles face more serious **persecution**, and many are imprisoned by the Jews. At midnight, an angel from the Lord sets them free. The apostles continue to teach people about Jesus.

[chapter 6]

1. The Church grows, and the leadership increases to include seven wise men, full of the Holy Spirit. They are chosen to free up the Apostles to "give their attention to **prayer** and the ministry of the Word."

2. One of the seven elders, **Stephen**, is seized by the Jews and falsely accused.

[chapter 7]

1. Stephen gives a sermon about the Gospel. He gives them a quick **history** of Israel to prove that Jesus was sent from God.

2. Because the Jewish leaders are "stiff-necked," they become angry at Stephen's speech and stone him to death.

[chapter 8]

1. On the day of Stephen's death, a "great persecution" breaks out in Jerusalem. This actually works for the good, because this causes the believers to **scatter** throughout "Judea and Samaria," bringing the message of the Gospel with them.

> **SAMARITANS:**
> A race of people who were only part Jewish. Many Jews during this time treated Samaritans with contempt.

2. Phillip goes to **Samaria** and preaches the Gospel.

3. One person, Simon, completely misunderstands the message, and offers to **buy** the power of the Holy Spirit.

4. Phillip meets an Ethiopian political leader and tells him about **Jesus**. The Ethiopian believes, and is baptized.

[chapter 9]

1. Saul (Paul) is converted to faith in Jesus. Prior to the conversion, he was a Jewish leader whose job was to persecute Christians. Many Christians are **afraid** of him.

2. While Saul is walking on the road, a light came from Heaven, God speaks to him, and then temporarily **blinds** him. After three days, a Christian named Ananias comes to Saul and heals him. Saul (Paul) begins to grow in the Lord.

3. As Peter is traveling about the country, he heals two more people and continues to **preach** the message of the Gospel.

[chapter 10]

1. In a vision, God tells Cornelius to send for Peter to come to his house. Cornelius was a Roman centurion and a **Gentile** who feared God (which means he likely attended Jewish prayer groups, or was a donor to a Jewish synagogue). He sends his servants to get Peter.

2. While the servants are coming to get Peter, Peter also has a **vision** from God. God repeats the vision three times to make sure Peter gets the point: "all foods are clean."

There are some that only chew the cud or only have a split hoof, but you must not eat them. The camel, though it chews the cud, does not have a split hoof; it is ceremonially unclean for you. The coney [rock badger], though it chews the cud, does not have a split hoof; it is unclean for you. The rabbit, though it chews the cud, does not have a split hoof; it is unclean for you. And the pig, though it has a split hoof completely divided, does not chew the cud; it is unclean for you. You must not eat their meat or touch their carcasses; they are unclean for you (Leviticus 11:4-8).

It was Old Testament laws like this which kept the Jews separate from other peoples. Often a Jew would not even go into a Gentile's house because it was "unclean."

Through Peter's vision, God declares all things, and all people, clean.

3. Peter goes to Cornelius' house and tells the whole household about Jesus. They believe and are **baptized** by the Holy Spirit.

[chapter 11]

1. When Peter gets back to Jerusalem, the apostles are amazed that the Gentiles have received the Holy Spirit. This goes beyond their understanding of grace and **salvation**. Even the apostles had serious misconceptions about how broad the Gospel message truly was.

2. Because of the persecution related to Stephen's death, the Church really starts to **spread** out and grow, especially in Antioch.

[chapter 12]

1. King Herod begins his own **persecution** of the Christians and puts some of them to death. When he sees that this **pleases** the Jews, he arrests Peter and plans to put him to death.

2. The Church responds in **prayer**:
So Peter was kept in prison, but the church was earnestly praying to God for him (Acts 12:5).

3. The night before his trial, an angel comes and frees Peter from jail. This **miracle** astonishes the Apostles.

4. Later, the people call Herod a god, and he didn't disagree with them. He quickly dies because he accepts that praise from men, and doesn't give **credit** to God.

[chapter 13 (see the end of this lesson for a map)]

1. Barnabus and **Saul** are commissioned by the local church, and soon set off for the first missionary journey.

2. They leave from Antioch to the port city of Seleucia. They then **sail** to the island of Cyprus, where they preach to the Jews first and then later to the Roman authorities.

3. Paul and his companions travel to Pisidian Antioch, where they preach in the synagogue. The Jews **reject** the message, so Paul preaches to the Gentiles. Persecution comes against Paul, so they leave for Iconium.

[chapter 14]

1. In Iconium, many Jews and Gentiles **believe**. The persecution starts up again, so Paul is forced to leave and go to Lystra.

2. Paul heals a cripple in Lystra and the people believe he is the Greek god Hermes. Paul **argues** strongly against this, and uses the opportunity to preach the Gospel.

3. Some Jews from Iconium come to Lystra and "won the crowd over." The crowd **stones** Paul, but he survives and leaves to preach the good news in another city, Derbe.

4. Many people in Derbe believe. Paul and his companions return home after **planting** many churches, and tell the disciples the good news of their successful trip.

[chapter 15 (see end of this lesson for a map)]

1. A big problem arises for the early church: Should Gentile Christians have to follow the Jewish laws? The church in Jerusalem said that Gentiles had to follow **the law** of Moses.

2. Paul and Barnabus go down to Jerusalem to set things straight. Their argument is simple: Salvation comes by faith, so observance of the law is **obsolete**. (Though for Jewish Christians, some allowance is given so as not to offend other Jews . . . but not as a prerequisite for salvation.)

3. The Council agreed that Gentiles were free from the Mosaic law, but urged them to avoid practices which would unnecessarily **offend** the Jews.

4. With the controversy settled, Paul takes off on his second missionary journey to "**visit** the brothers in all the towns where [they] preached the gospel" (15:36).

5. There is a division between Paul and Barnabas over the usefulness of John Mark (Mark). It splits up the team. Paul takes Silas with him, and Barnabas takes John Mark and heads another direction. God used their disagreement to double their efforts in spreading the Gospel.

[chapter 16]

1. Paul goes to Derbe and then Lystra where he meets **Timothy**, a believer he takes with him to train and disciple him further.

2. Luke joins Paul, and they go to Macedonia. Paul's **pattern** remains the same: he preached first to the Jews, and then to the Gentiles.

3. In Macedonia, Paul casts a demon out of a girl and then is thrown in jail for doing so. This time, to get him out of jail, God sends a great earthquake. Even in jail, Paul preaches the Gospel to his **captors**.

[chapter 17]

1. Paul goes to Thessalonica, and preaches in the synagogue for three weeks. The Jews get angry and form a mob to **kill** him.

2. Paul leaves quickly and goes to the people of Berea, who are of "more noble character." Many Jews and Gentiles **accepted** Jesus. However, angry Jews from Thessalonica come and force Paul to leave.

3. Paul travels to Athens, and is "greatly distressed" because the people worship so many **idols**. But Paul shifts gears and brings his message to his new kind of listener.

Preaching to a **philosopher** would require a specific approach. For example, a philosopher would not care about an Old Testament prophecy.

Paul did not change the **message** of the Gospel, he changed his methods for presenting the Gospel.

[chapter 18 (see end of this lesson for a map)]

The Church continues to grow in every area where the Gospel is preached. Paul spends a year-and-a-half in Corinth. Paul trains up new **leaders** and visits many of the churches he started (third missionary trip).

[chapter 19]

Paul spends over two years in Ephesus, and sees some extraordinary success with people accepting the Gospel. However, it is not universally accepted, and there is a huge riot in Ephesus. Eventually, it is dismissed because the people who were rioting are told they should take it to the **courts**.

[chapter 20]

1. Paul travels some more in Macedonia. In Troas, Paul preaches such a long sermon, one man falls **asleep** and then falls to his death three stories from a window sill. Paul goes downstairs and heals him, so he rises from the dead (and probably told him not to sleep during sermons again).

2. Paul gives a stirring farewell **speech** to the elders in Ephesus. (You should check it out!)

[chapter 21]

1. On the way home to Jerusalem, a prophet tells Paul that if he goes there, he is going to be **bound** and handed over to the Gentiles.

2. Paul returns to Jerusalem, where his **reputation** as a missionary for Christ has preceded him.
The elders of the Jerusalem church are overjoyed with the **success** that Paul has seen.
The Jewish leaders are furious with Paul because they believe he has been spreading **heresy** among the Jews. They seize Paul and a riot breaks out at the Temple. The Romans capture Paul to keep him from getting killed.

[chapter 22]

1. Paul speaks to the crowd in his defense. He gives them his Jewish credentials and his testimony of how he became a Christian. When he tells the crowd that he was sent by God to preach the message to the **Gentiles**, they go crazy and want to kill him.

2. Because Paul was a **Roman** citizen, the Romans release him.

[chapter 23]

1. The Roman commander calls together the Sanhedrin, trying to settle the matter **quickly**. Once again, Paul proclaims what he believes, and another riot takes place.

2. The Jews form a conspiracy to kill Paul but it is discovered. So Paul is **moved** to Caesarea to have his case heard by another ruler (Felix).

[chapter 24]

1. The Jewish leaders go to Caesarea to make their case. They say that Paul is a "trouble-maker, stirring up riots among the Jews all over the world. He is a **ringleader** of the Nazarene sect" (Acts 24:5).

2. Paul makes his defense: he cites several times when he didn't cause **riots**, and claims that he isn't subversive, but rather, that he follows the Old Testament Law.

3. Although Paul is not guilty, Felix keeps him in prison for **two** years.

[chapter 25]

1. Paul goes to trial again, and he knows he is not going to get a fair one. If the trial progresses as planned, he will be handed over to the Jewish leaders (who will kill him). Paul **appeals** to have his case heard by Caesar, the Emperor. This is his right as a Roman citizen.

2. King Agrippa hears about all of this and wants to **talk** to Paul before he is sent to Caesar.

[chapter 26]

1. Paul, once again, is given the opportunity to defend himself against his accusers, the Jewish leaders. He gives his life testimony: he was a Pharisee, converted to faith in Jesus, and was **obedient** to his call to preach to the Gentiles.

[chapter 27]

1. Paul and his companions set sail for Rome. On the way they run into a huge **storm** that causes the ship to wreck. Everyone on board has to swim to shore.

2. On the island (modern day Malta), Paul is bitten by a poisonous snake yet doesn't die. After healing all of the sick people on the island and waiting **three** months for winter to end, Paul sets off for Rome.

[chapter 28]

1. Paul arrives in Rome and is greeted by many Christians who have heard about his coming. Paul is allowed to live by **himself**, but under guard.

2. Paul slips into his usual obedient-to-God habits; he tells everyone about the Gospel message, first the **Jews**, and then the Gentiles.

For two whole years Paul stayed there in his own rented house and welcomed all who came to see him. Boldly and without hindrance he preached the kingdom of God and taught about the Lord Jesus Christ (28:30-31).

PERSONAL BIBLE STUDY #1: HOLY SPIRIT IN THE BOOK OF ACTS

Take some time on your own to read through the following verses. Take notes on what they teach about the Holy Spirit. If a verse seems confusing, look up the reference in your Bible and read the surrounding context. If it is still difficult to understand, make a note and ask your leader about it. Remember, this isn't a race, work through these verses at your own pace. Don't forget to start with prayer!

Acts 1:2 - . . . until the day he was taken up to heaven, after giving instructions through the Holy Spirit to the apostles he had chosen.

Acts 1:5 - "For John baptized with water, but in a few days you will be baptized with the Holy Spirit."

Acts 1:8 - "But you will receive power when the Holy Spirit comes on you; and you will be my witnesses in Jerusalem, in all Judea and Samaria, and to the ends of the earth."

Acts 1:16 - "Friends, the scripture had to be fulfilled, which the Holy Spirit through David foretold concerning Judas, who became a guide for those who arrested Jesus . . ."

Acts 2:4 - All of them were filled with the Holy Spirit and began to speak in other tongues as the Spirit enabled them.

Acts 2:17 - In the last days, God says, I will pour out my Spirit on all people. Your sons and daughters will prophesy, your young men will see visions, your old men will dream dreams.

Acts 2:18 – Even on my servants, both men and women, I will pour out my Spirit in those days, and they will prophesy.

Acts 2:33 - Exalted to the right hand of God, he has received from the Father the promised Holy Spirit and has poured out what you now see and hear.

Acts 2:38 - Peter replied, "Repent and be baptized, every one of you, in the name of Jesus Christ for the forgiveness of your sins. And you will receive the gift of the Holy Spirit."

Acts 4:8 - Then Peter, filled with the Holy Spirit, said to them: "Rulers and elders of the people!"

Acts 4:25 - You spoke by the Holy Spirit through the mouth of your servant, our father David: "Why do the nations rage and the peoples plot in vain?"

Acts 4:31 - After they prayed, the place where they were meeting was shaken. And they were all filled with the Holy Spirit and spoke the word of God boldly.

Acts 5:3 - Then Peter said, "Ananias, how is it that Satan has so filled your heart that you have lied to the Holy Spirit and have kept for yourself some of the money you received for the land?"

Acts 5:9 - Peter said to her, "How could you agree to test the Spirit of the Lord? Look! The feet of the men who buried your husband are at the door, and they will carry you out also."

Acts 5:32 - "We are witnesses of these things, and so is the Holy Spirit, whom God has given to those who obey him."

Acts 6:3 - "Brothers, choose seven men from among you who are known to be full of the Spirit and wisdom. We will turn this responsibility over to them . . ."

Acts 6:5 - This proposal pleased the whole group. They chose Stephen, a man full of faith and of the Holy Spirit; also Philip, Procorus, Nicanor, Timon, Parmenas, and Nicolas from Antioch, a convert to Judaism.

Acts 6:10 - . . . but they could not stand up against his wisdom or the Spirit by whom he spoke.

Acts 7:51 - "You stiff-necked people, with uncircumcised hearts and ears! You are just like your fathers: You always resist the Holy Spirit!"

Acts 7:55 - But Stephen, full of the Holy Spirit, looked up to heaven and saw the glory of God, and Jesus standing at the right hand of God.

Acts 7:59 - While they were stoning him, Stephen prayed, "Lord Jesus, receive my spirit."

Acts 8:15 - When they arrived, they prayed for them that they might receive the Holy Spirit . . .

Acts 8:16 - . . . because the Holy Spirit had not yet come upon any of them; they had simply been baptized into[c] the name of the Lord Jesus.

Acts 8:17 - Then Peter and John placed their hands on them, and they received the Holy Spirit.

Acts 8:18 - When Simon saw that the Spirit was given at the laying on of the apostles' hands, he offered them money . . .

Acts 8:19 - . . . and said, "Give me also this ability so that everyone on whom I lay my hands may receive the Holy Spirit."

Acts 8:29 - The Spirit told Philip, "Go to that chariot and stay near it."

Acts 8:39 - When they came up out of the water, the Spirit of the Lord suddenly took Philip away, and the eunuch did not see him again, but went on his way rejoicing.

Acts 9:17 - Then Ananias went to the house and entered it. Placing his hands on Saul, he said, "Brother Saul, the Lord—Jesus, who appeared to you on the road as you were coming here—has sent me so that you may see again and be filled with the Holy Spirit."

Acts 9:31 - Then the church throughout Judea, Galilee and Samaria enjoyed a time of peace. It was strengthened; and encouraged by the Holy Spirit, it grew in numbers, living in the fear of the Lord.

Acts 10:19 - While Peter was still thinking about the vision, the Spirit said to him, "Simon, three men are looking for you.

Acts 10:38 - . . . how God anointed Jesus of Nazareth with the Holy Spirit and power, and how he went around doing good and healing all who were under the power of the devil, because God was with him.

Acts 10:44 - While Peter was still speaking these words, the Holy Spirit came on all who heard the message.

Acts 10:45 - The circumcised believers who had come with Peter were astonished that the gift of the Holy Spirit had been poured out even on the Gentiles.

Acts 10:47 - "Can anyone keep these people from being baptized with water? They have received the Holy Spirit just as we have."

Acts 11:12 - The Spirit told me to have no hesitation about going with them. These six brothers also went with me, and we entered the man's house.

Acts 11:15 - "As I began to speak, the Holy Spirit came on them as he had come on us at the beginning."

Acts 11:16 - "Then I remembered what the Lord had said: 'John baptized with water, but you will be baptized with the Holy Spirit.'"

Acts 11:24 - He was a good man, full of the Holy Spirit and faith, and a great number of people were brought to the Lord.

Acts 11:28 - One of them, named Agabus, stood up and through the Spirit predicted that a severe famine would spread over the entire Roman world. (This happened during the reign of Claudius.)

Acts 13:2 - While they were worshiping the Lord and fasting, the Holy Spirit said, "Set apart for me Barnabas and Saul for the work to which I have called them."

Acts 13:4 - The two of them, sent on their way by the Holy Spirit, went down to Seleucia and sailed from there to Cyprus.

Acts 13:9 - Then Saul, who was also called Paul, filled with the Holy Spirit, looked straight at Elymas . . .

Acts 13:52 - And the disciples were filled with joy and with the Holy Spirit.

Acts 15:8 - God, who knows the heart, showed that he accepted them by giving the Holy Spirit to them, just as he did to us.

Acts 15:28 - It seemed good to the Holy Spirit and to us not to burden you with anything beyond the following requirements . . .

Acts 16:6 - Paul and his companions traveled throughout the region of Phrygia and Galatia, having been kept by the Holy Spirit from preaching the word in the province of Asia.

Acts 16:7 - When they came to the border of Mysia, they tried to enter Bithynia, but the Spirit of Jesus would not allow them to.

Acts 16:16 - Once when we were going to the place of prayer, we were met by a slave girl who had a spirit by which she predicted the future. She earned a great deal of money for her owners by fortune-telling.

Acts 16:18 - She kept this up for many days. Finally Paul became so troubled that he turned around and said to the spirit, "In the name of Jesus Christ I command you to come out of her!" At that moment the spirit left her.

Acts 19:2 - There he found some disciples and asked them, "Did you receive the Holy Spirit when you believed?" They answered, "No, we have not even heard that there is a Holy Spirit."

Acts 19:6 - When Paul placed his hands on them, the Holy Spirit came on them, and they spoke in tongues and prophesied.

Acts 19:15 - (One day) the evil spirit answered them, "Jesus I know, and I know about Paul, but who are you?"

Acts 19:16 - Then the man who had the evil spirit jumped on them and overpowered them all. He gave them such a beating that they ran out of the house naked and bleeding.

Acts 19:21 - After all this had happened, Paul decided to go to Jerusalem, passing through Macedonia and Achaia. "After I have been there," he said, "I must visit Rome also."

Acts 20:22 - "And now, compelled by the Spirit, I am going to Jerusalem, not knowing what will happen to me there."

Acts 20:23 - I only know that in every city the Holy Spirit warns me that prison and hardships are facing me.

Acts 20:28 - Keep watch over yourselves and all the flock of which the Holy Spirit has made you overseers. Be shepherds of the church of God, which he bought with his own blood.

Acts 21:4 - Finding the disciples there, we stayed with them seven days. Through the Spirit they urged Paul not to go on to Jerusalem.

Acts 21:11 - Coming over to us, he took Paul's belt, tied his own hands and feet with it and said, "The Holy Spirit says, 'In this way the Jews of Jerusalem will bind the owner of this belt and will hand him over to the Gentiles.' "

Acts 23:8 - (The Sadducees say that there is no resurrection, and that there are neither angels nor spirits, but the Pharisees acknowledge them all.)

Acts 23:9 - There was a great uproar, and some of the teachers of the law who were Pharisees stood up and argued vigorously. "We find nothing wrong with this man," they said. "What if a spirit or an angel has spoken to him?"

Acts 28:25 - They disagreed among themselves and began to leave after Paul had made this final statement: "The Holy Spirit spoke the truth to your forefathers when he said through Isaiah the prophet . . .

PERSONAL BIBLE STUDY #2: BAPTISM IN ACTS

Take some time on your own to read through the following verses. Take notes on what they teach about baptism. If a verse seems confusing, look up the reference in your Bible and read the surrounding context. If it is still difficult to understand, make a note and ask your leader about it. Remember, this isn't a race, work through these verses at your own pace. Don't forget to start with prayer!

Acts 1:5 - For John baptized with water, but in a few days you will be baptized with the Holy Spirit."

Acts 1:22 - ". . . beginning from John's baptism to the time when Jesus was taken up from us. For one of these must become a witness with us of his resurrection."

Acts 2:38 - Peter replied, "Repent and be baptized, every one of you, in the name of Jesus Christ for the forgiveness of your sins. And you will receive the gift of the Holy Spirit."

Acts 2:41 - Those who accepted his message were baptized, and about three thousand were added to their number that day.

Acts 8:12 - But when they believed Philip as he preached the good news of the kingdom of God and the name of Jesus Christ, they were baptized, both men and women.

Acts 8:13 - Simon himself believed and was baptized. And he followed Philip everywhere, astonished by the great signs and miracles he saw.

Acts 8:16 - . . . because the Holy Spirit had not yet come upon any of them; they had simply been baptized into the name of the Lord Jesus.

Acts 8:36 - As they traveled along the road, they came to some water and the eunuch said, "Look, here is water. Why shouldn't I be baptized?"

Acts 8:38 - And he gave orders to stop the chariot. Then both Philip and the eunuch went down into the water and Philip baptized him.

Acts 9:18 - Immediately, something like scales fell from Saul's eyes, and he could see again. He got up and was baptized . . .

Acts 10:37 - You know what has happened throughout Judea, beginning in Galilee after the baptism that John preached . . .

Acts 10:47 - "Can anyone keep these people from being baptized with water? They have received the Holy Spirit just as we have."

Acts 10:48 - So he ordered that they be baptized in the name of Jesus Christ. Then they asked Peter to stay with them for a few days.

Acts 11:16 - "Then I remembered what the Lord had said: 'John baptized with water, but you will be baptized with the Holy Spirit.'"

Acts 13:24 - "Before the coming of Jesus, John preached repentance and baptism to all the people of Israel."

Acts 16:15 - When she and the members of her household were baptized, she invited us to her home. "If you consider me a believer in the Lord," she said, "come and stay at my house." And she persuaded us.

Acts 16:33 - At that hour of the night the jailer took them and washed their wounds; then immediately he and all his family were baptized.

Acts 18:8 - Crispus, the synagogue ruler, and his entire household believed in the Lord; and many of the Corinthians who heard him believed and were baptized.

Acts 18:25 - He had been instructed in the way of the Lord, and he spoke with great fervor and taught about Jesus accurately, though he knew only the baptism of John.

Acts 19:3 - So Paul asked, "Then what baptism did you receive?" "John's baptism," they replied.

Acts 19:4 - Paul said, "John's baptism was a baptism of repentance. He told the people to believe in the one coming after him, that is, in Jesus."

Acts 19:5 - On hearing this, they were baptized into the name of the Lord Jesus.

Acts 22:16 - "'And now what are you waiting for? Get up, be baptized and wash your sins away, calling on his name.'"

MAP: PAUL'S FIRST MISSIONARY TRIP

Norris, D. T. Logos Deluxe Map Set. Oak Harbor, WA: Logos Research Systems, Inc., 1997 © 1995.

MAP: PAUL'S SECOND MISSIONARY TRIP

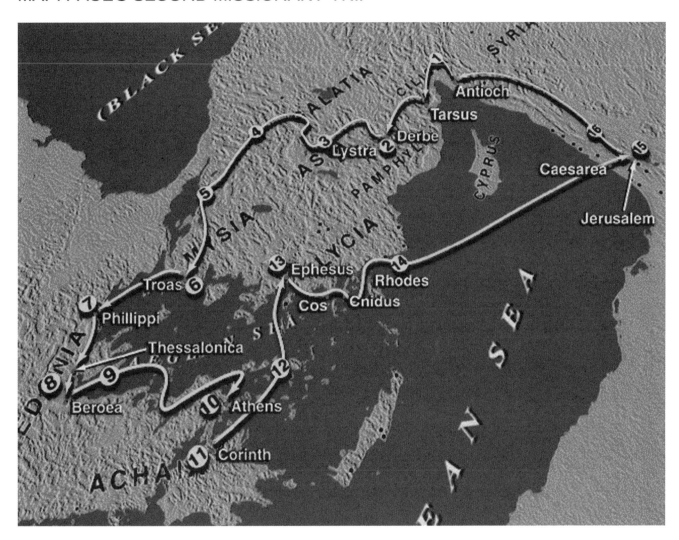

Norris, D. T. *Logos Deluxe Map Set.* Oak Harbor, WA: Logos Research Systems, Inc., 1997 © 1995.

MAP: PAUL'S THIRD MISSIONARY TRIP

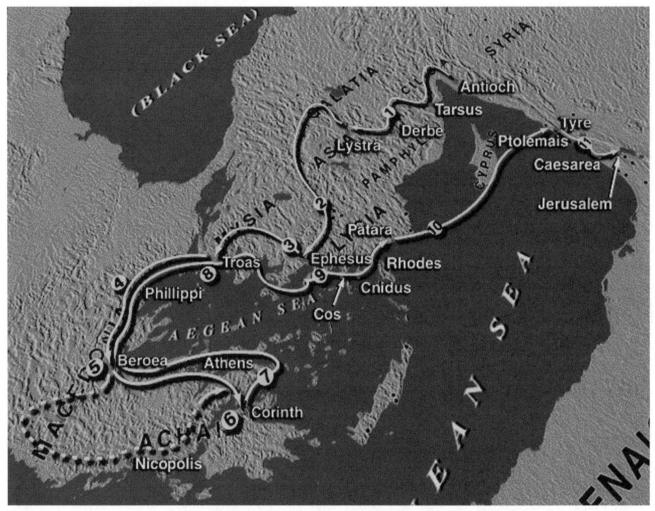

Norris, D. T. Logos Deluxe Map Set. Oak Harbor, WA: Logos Research Systems, Inc., 1997 © 1995.

THE LETTERS OF PAUL

ROOTED:NEW TESTAMENT

ROOTED : NEW TESTAMENT

study five the letters of paul

TABLE OF CONTENTS

INTRODUCTION

The New Testament can roughly be organized into three parts:

   (a) The Gospels and Acts

   (b) The Letters

   (c) The Apocalypse (Revelation)

Of the 27 books in the New Testament, __13__ were written by one man: Paul. Before we look at Paul's letters, it is important to first take a quick look at his __life__. To understand and interpret Paul's letters, they cannot be divorced from the __context__ in which they were written.

A SHORT BACKGROUND OF PAUL

[paul's life before Christ]

1. Paul, whose name used to Saul, was born in the Greek city of Tarsus (in what is today southeastern Turkey). His mother was Jewish and his father was a __Roman__ citizen.

2. In his early youth, Paul was sent to Jerusalem to become a student of the Jewish laws. His teacher, Gamaliel, was a very famous __Rabbi__ (see Acts 22:3).

3. At some point in his life, Paul also learned the trade of __tent__ making. Every Jewish Rabbi was expected to learn a practical trade (Acts 18:3; 1 Thessalonians 2:9).

4. Paul was a zealous Jew, eager to live according to strict moral laws. When the Church came into existence, Paul was quick to begin persecution of what he saw as a __perversion__ of the Jewish faith. Stephen was the first Christian martyr put to death for his faith, and his execution was under the approval and direction of Paul (Acts 8:1).

5. On his way to persecuting the Christians at Damascus, Paul was struck __blind__ by Jesus who asked, "Why do you persecute me?" This event was so important to Paul's life that Luke mentions it three times in the book of Acts (9:3-19; 22:6-16; 26:9-23).

6. After his conversion, Paul began to preach the Gospel of Jesus **boldly** to non-believers.

7. In summary, it is important to understand Paul as:

(a) Roman citizen: he was familiar with Hellenistic language, culture, and government; he made several appeals to his citizenship during his journeys (Acts journeys - Acts 16:37; 22:25; 25:11).

(b) Pharisee: Jewish sect which emphasized obedience to Jewish Law (Mosaic Law, combined with tradition).

(c) Apostle of Jesus: the death and resurrection of Jesus forced Paul to reinterpret his vast understanding of the Old Testament.

[paul the apostle]

1. Most of Paul's life as an Apostle was spent **traveling** great distances to preach the Gospel. After his conversion, his life consisted mostly of three missionary journeys and his trip to Rome as a prisoner.

(At the end of this lesson, there is a list of cities Paul visited on his three missionary journeys, as well as a short chronology of Paul's life.)

2. Paul started many churches but did not stay at any one church for a long period of time. Although he tried to **visit** them as often as he could, it wasn't enough; the churches had many questions and problems.

3. Thus, as Paul traveled the world preaching, he also wrote many letters to the churches to encourage and **instruct**.

4. The letters of Paul that survived were collected and are in the New Testament.
   (a) They are: Romans, 1 & 2 Corinthians, Galatians, Ephesians, Philippians, Colossians, 1 & 2 Thessalonians, 1 & 2 Timothy, Titus, Philemon.

   (b) His letters are arranged roughly by size, largest to smallest.

   (c) Chronologically, his letters were probably written in the following order: Galatians, 1 & 2 Thessalonians, 1 & 2 Corinthians, Romans, Philemon, Colossians, Ephesians, 1 Timothy, Titus, 2 Timothy.

THE ANCIENT LETTER

Paul's writings aren't technically **letters**; they belong to a genre (type) of literature called an "epistle."

    (a) Letter: private communication, written to one person.

    (b) Epistle: public communication, more official, written to a group.

[some characteristics]

1. Epistles were common in the ancient world. They were generally written by a **scribe** called an "amanuensus." The author would normally dictate his letter to the scribe.

    (a) This process usually isn't word for word; rather, the scribe took **notes** and wrote out the actual text at a later time.

    (b) If the author was intending for his work to be **circulated** to many groups (as Paul certainly was) he would carefully review the final product.

2. The term epistle is used to describe a body of literature that fits into a similar **form** and structure. Aside from lengthening his epistles, Paul wrote them according to the same rules as his contemporaries:

    (a) name of the **writer** and recipient;

Paul, a servant of Christ Jesus, called to be an apostle and set apart for the gospel of God . . . . To all in Rome who are loved by God and called to be saints (Romans 1:1, 7a).

    (b) some **greeting** wishing peace for the recipient;

Grace and peace to you from God our Father and from the Lord Jesus Christ (Romans 1:7b).

    (c) polite expression of **thanks** for the good health for the recipient. Paul expanded this to give thanks to God;
First, I thank my God through Jesus Christ for all of you, because your faith is being reported all over the world (Romans 1:8).

    (d) main body of letter (Paul's epistles are considerably **longer** than their ancient counterparts);

    (e) personal **news**;

But now that there is no more place for me to work in these regions, and since I have been longing for many years to see you, I plan to do so when I go to Spain. I hope to visit you while passing through and to have you assist me on my journey there, after I have enjoyed your company for a while (Romans 15:23-24).

(f) exhortation or **blessing**;

I urge you, brothers, to watch out for those who cause divisions and put obstacles in your way that are contrary to the teaching you have learned. Keep away from them (Romans 16:17).

(g) ends with a word of farewell, which Paul usually expanded to a **prayer**.

Now to him who is able to establish you by my gospel and the proclamation of Jesus Christ, according to the revelation of the mystery hidden for long ages past (Romans 16:25).

[reading the epistles]

There are a few things to keep in mind when reading Paul's epistles:
(a) They were written to encourage and instruct believers at the **churches** he started.

(b) They were read **publicly** and were meant to be circulated to the surrounding churches, even when they were addressed to an individual.

(c) They were written to a specific audience and, thus, addressed specific **situations** (occasions).
    (i) Reading the epistle is like listening to one side of a phone conversation. Most of the conversation would be easy to understand, but some would be difficult because we can't hear what the other person is **saying**. To add to the difficulties, we don't know what knowledge both sides share.

    (ii) The Corinthians had different problems and questions from the Thessalonians, and thus Paul wrote different letters to each group.

    (iii) Because each epistle came out of a specific occasion, Paul had a specific **purpose** for each of his writings. There is a very close relationship between occasion and purpose.

[occasion]

Events which proceed and create the historical context and motive for writing. (e.g. The Galatian church was listening to false teachers called "Judaizers.")

[purpose]

The main point(s) the author seeks to communicate in his writing (e.g. In his letter to the Galatians, Paul argues against the Judaizers by teaching the true purpose and function of the Law.)

The epistles are not theological textbooks. Even Paul's greatest epistle—**Romans**—is not a textbook of systematic theology. Context is all-important for interpretation.

2. Paul always made a close **connection** between the theology of Christ and moral/ethical regulations for the believer (see Romans 12:1; Ephesians 4:1; Philippians 2:12; Colossians 3:5).

3. One of Paul's greatest theological struggles was centered on the concepts of **grace** and **law**. His struggle was not in understanding these things, but in communicating them to others.

   Grace: God's free gift of salvation.

   Law: God's perfect commandments for his people.

   (a) How did the Jews respond to this? They saw Paul as "throwing away" God's Word as revealed in the only Scriptures they had—the Old Testament.

   (b) How did the Gentiles respond to this? They saw Paul as requiring strict obedience, though the Jerusalem Counsel (Acts 15) relieved the pressure to become a Jew before becoming a Christian.

4. Understanding the tension between grace and law.

   (a) In the life of a believer, accepting God's grace and obeying God's law **follow** one another. They are both extremely important.

   (b) The devil works hard to **twist** the truth. Misunderstanding truth causes more harm than ignorance.

   The truth: salvation is by faith through grace; evidence of a salvation ought to be a changed life, which is living in obedience to God's law.

5. Advanced study of the epistles will yield the differences in **styles**, even among Paul's letters. (e.g. The pastoral epistles contain a slightly different vocabulary from most of Paul's other works.)

6. This is clearly due to the use of different **scribes**. Scribes were often used in ancient times. Paul dictated most (if not all) of his letters and a scribe wrote them out.

ROMANS

Paul wrote this letter to the Church in **Rome** from the city of Corinth near the end of his third missionary journey.

[occasion]

Paul had spent a considerable amount of time preaching the Gospel in many of the strategic centers of population in the known Mediterranean world. Rome was the capital, and if the gospel could be **planted** there, it would undoubtedly have far reaching effects. Paul had not yet been to Rome.

[purpose]

Paul clearly intended this epistle to prepare the Church in Rome for his visit. This epistle contains Paul's most detailed description and explanation of the Gospel. Paul wanted to make sure the Church in Rome had a **complete** and full understanding of the Gospel. He didn't start this church, so perhaps he wasn't confident in their understanding of the major tenets of the faith.

Paul was already feeling the **pressure** of persecution (e.g. Corinth, Acts 20:3) and he might not have been sure that he would live to get the chance to preach the Gospel west of Greece.

Romans is by far the greatest and most **comprehensive** of Paul's works, laying out the truths of salvation in an orderly manner.

(a) Chapters 1–8, in short, teach that all people are **sinners**; salvation comes from faith through God's grace; and that salvation leads to a changed lifestyle.

(b) Chapters 9–11 deal with the relationship between **salvation** and the Jews.

(c) Chapters 12–16 provide some practical guidelines for **living** the Christian life.

1 CORINTHIANS

Paul wrote this epistle sometime after his **first** visit to Corinth, while he was in the city of Ephesus (on his third missionary journey).

[occasion]

Paul had just received a report from "Chloe's household," and a letter from the Church itself, which contained some specific **questions** (1 Corinthians 1:11, 7:1).

[purpose]

Paul wrote this first letter to **correct** some serious doctrinal and moral sins (things that were dividing the Church). First Corinthians is an excellent, practical document teaching about the daily living of individual Christians, corporate worship, and other key issues.

2 CORINTHIANS

Paul wrote this epistle to the Church in Corinth when he was in Philippi (Macedonia).

Several events **happened** between 1 and 2 Corinthians that will be helpful to highlight.
- **Spring**
   55 A.D.
   1 Corinthians was written, and the church responded well and made **changes**.

- **Summer/Fall**
   55 A.D.
   Conditions turned bad, and Paul had to make a "**painful** visit" (12:14, 13:1).

- **Spring**
   56 A.D.
   Paul wrote a "**severe** letter" (lost) (2:3-9; 7-8, 12).

- **Summer**
   56 A.D.
   Titus arrived in Macedonia to **update** Paul on conditions in the Corinthian church.

Titus had returned to Paul and reported that the Corinthians responded well to the "**severe letter**." Some time after Titus' report, disturbing news about the church in Corinth arrived.

[purpose]

to **express** delight/relief at the Corinthians positive response to the "severe letter";
to **remind** the church to complete their collection of relief money to help the Christians in Jerusalem;
to **prepare** them for his upcoming visit by having them engage in self-examination.

GALATIANS

Paul wrote this to the "**churches** in Galatia" from the city of Antioch.

There is very little agreement as to who the Galatians actually were. This is **debated** widely among scholars. The term "Galatia" could refer to two different things: (1) an ethnic group, or (2) a province created by the Romans. Paul visited both, so either could be possible.

(a) Northern theory: the original territory held by an ethnic group.

(b) Southern theory: the Romans created a province which was further south.

[occasion]

Christianity was just beginning to take root in the Gentile world because the earliest church members were Jewish. An important problem arose: Would Gentiles have to take on Jewish cultural and religious **practices**, such as circumcision?

This debate held some serious consequences for Christian **unity** because the answer would turn out to be the key on the theology of salvation.

[purpose]

Paul answered this debate with a loud **NO**! Salvation is by faith in Christ. Paul begins his argument by laying down his credentials as an Apostle called by God, preaching the one true Gospel. Even the Jewish Apostles (Peter and James) extended to Paul the "right hand of fellowship" (2:9). He had the authority to teach the true Gospel.

Paul teaches that if a person follows the Mosaic law, it will lead to spiritual **death**. Salvation is only through God's grace. Although the cornerstone of Christianity is by faith, Paul explains the meaning of Christian freedom:

You, my brothers, were called to be free. But do not use your freedom to indulge the sinful nature; rather, serve one another in love (Galatians 5:13).

EPHESIANS

Paul wrote this epistle to the church in Ephesus while he was **imprisoned** in Rome.

[occasion]

Although Paul was in prison, it was more like "house arrest," which allowed him to receive **visitors**. Paul had received a report from Epaphrus concerning several congregations. One of Paul's representatives, Tychicus (a native of Ephesus), was about to leave Rome for Ephesus. Paul sent with him three letters: Colossians, Philemon, and Ephesians.

Paul started the church in Ephesus on the way home from his second missionary journey. He only stayed for a brief time. However, on his third missionary journey he stayed in Ephesus for more than three years (Acts 20:3). Ephesus was the **hub** of a huge province, its "rim" contained 236 independent communities. Although Paul spent his time in Ephesus, the Gospel soon spread to the surrounding communities.

[purpose]

This letter was especially intended for general circulation and does not deal with particular church issues. Paul uses this letter to explain the **fellowship** Christians are to have within the Church. Although most of the major Pauline themes are reflected in the epistle, its main theme is the unity of believers, which comes through Christ.

This unity includes not only the Church, but will also include all **creation** at the end of time.

PHILIPPIANS

Paul wrote this epistle to the Church in Philippi while he was imprisoned in Rome. Philippians seem to be separate from the other prison epistles (Ephesians, Colossians, Philemon), because it was carried by a different **messenger**.

[occasion]

While in prison, the Philippian church sent a messenger, Epaphroditus, to Paul with a gift. Epaphroditus was also sent to minister to Paul's needs and doubtless he brought news of the Church's **progress**.

During the course of his ministry, Epaphroditus became gravely ill and almost **died**. When he got better, he went home and Paul sent this epistle with him.

[purpose]

Rejoice in the Lord always. I will say it again: Rejoice! (Philippians 4:4)

Of all the letters Paul wrote to churches, Philippians stands out as the most **personal**. Paul had no sharp words of rebuke, only encouragement. This epistle screams joy to the reader. Although Paul is in chains and some are preaching the Gospel with bad motives, he still is filled with joy. He wants the Philippians to also be filled with joy—no matter what!

COLOSSIANS

Paul wrote this epistle to the Church in Colossae, while he was imprisoned in Rome. There is no record (in Acts or otherwise) of the **establishment** of this church. Although it was a hundred miles from Ephesus, Colossae was probably evangelized during Paul's extended stay (Acts 19:10).

[occasion]

As mentioned above (Ephesians: Occasion), the arrival of Epaphras to Rome brought Paul news about many churches. Apparently, Colossae had some **heretical** teachers. Although difficult to ascertain with any certainty, the "Colossian Heresy" consisted of three elements:

Colossian Heresy:
  (a) Jewish Element: legalism; observance of holy days.

  (b) Pagan Element: early gnosticism; the belief that all physical things were evil; salvation came through knowledge; worship of many gods.

  (c) Christian Element: really more a "mask" than a true element; this heresy did not deny Christ, but it dethroned Him.

[purpose]

Paul wrote Colossians to:

(a) express his interest in the Church

(b) to warn them against returning to their old **ways**; and

(c) to refute the so-called Colossian Heresy.

1 THESSALONIANS

Paul wrote this epistle to the church in Thessalonica from the city of Corinth.

[occasion]

Timothy returned from Thessalonica to Corinth with a **report** about their "faith and love" (3:6).

Timothy's report included:

(a) how well the church was standing in spite of persecution;

(b) that there were some people in the Church trying to undermine Paul's authority, reputation, and sincerity;

(c) that the Church was **confused** about what happened to the dead, and

(d) that some areas of their moral life needed improvement.

[purpose]

In response to Timothy's report, Paul sought to:

(a) express **thanks** to God for the Church's health;

(b) argue against those who sought to **undermine** his work;

(c) suggest some specific ways the Church could live **better lives**.

2 THESSALONIANS

Paul wrote this epistle shortly after his first letter to the church in Thessalonica. Paul was still in Corinth, and had received news of the Church's further **progress**.

[occasion]

Apparently, the persecution became much worse for the Church. The persecution was mixed with false teaching and this led to the belief that the **end times** were upon the Church. Since many believed the return of Christ was (very) near, people had begun to quit their jobs.

[purpose]

In response to the situation (occasion) in Thessalonica, Paul sought to:

   (a) encourage the Church to hang on through their persecutions;

   (b) correct their bad **theology** concerning the return of Christ, and

   (c) exhort the Church to keep away from people who quit their jobs.

THE PASTORAL EPISTLES

For this reason I am sending to you Timothy, my son whom I love, who is faithful in the Lord (1 Corinthians 4:17).

To Titus, my true son in our common faith (Titus 1:4).

1 Timothy, 2 Timothy, and Titus belong to a group of Paul's writings called the Pastoral Epistles. Timothy and Titus were two of Paul's "spiritual" sons who worked **alongside** Paul to spread the Gospel and encourage the Church.

These three works are closely related in their occasion and **purpose**. For this reason we will consider them together and then individually for their content and themes.

Paul wrote 1 Timothy and Titus after his first **imprisonment** in Rome, while he was in Macedonia visiting churches. Timothy was pastoring in Ephesus, and Titus was on the Island of Crete.

Paul wrote 2 Timothy during his second imprisonment in Rome, which would eventually end in his **execution**. It is assumed that Timothy was still in Ephesus.

[occasion and purpose]

The Pastoral Epistles provide a wealth of information concerning the practical side of running the **local church**.

Both Timothy and Titus are assumed to be **young**, therefore it appears that Paul's epistles provided encouragement and sound instruction.

They also helped to establish the **authority** of Timothy and Titus as Paul's chosen representatives.

Broadly understood, Paul outlines the pastoral responsibilities as two-fold:

   (a) defend sound doctrine, and

   (b) maintain **discipline**.

The Pastoral Epistles are highly **personal** in character and aren't very structured. They read more like a conversation that bounces around several topics.

1 TIMOTHY

Paul begins his first epistle to Timothy by warning him against **false** teachers. After thanking God for the amazing work He has done in his life, Paul moves on to some specific guidelines for worship, conduct, and church leadership.

In Chapter 4, Paul gives some personal instructions to Timothy, again warning him against false teachers. Then Paul deals with how special groups (widows, elders, etc.) were to be **treated**.

2 TIMOTHY

Paul's last epistle is much more personal than all his others. This is because it was written near the time of his **death**.

Paul urges Timothy to remain strong to his faith and strong in his **sufferings**. Paul warns yet again about false teachers and the need to be the Lord's servant. In the third chapter, Paul teaches about the last days and the godlessness they will bring. Then Paul gives his final **charge** to Timothy.

TITUS

Titus was in a place that was famous for its sinful, pleasure-seeking lifestyle. Paul knew this and wrote Titus to encourage and re-establish him as pastor. Paul lays down some guidelines for church leadership (similar to what he did with Timothy) and warns him to refute the false teachers. Then Paul gives several instructions concerning living a godly lifestyle. Of the three Pastoral Epistles, Paul stresses Christian **conduct** the most in Titus.

PHILEMON

Paul wrote this letter to a **slave owner**, Philemon, owner of the slave Onesimus.

[occasion]

Philemon was a Christian who had some relationship with Paul. One of his slaves, Onesimus, **ran away** (a crime punishable by death). Onesimus ran into Paul and became a believer. Some time later, Paul sent Onesimus back to Philemon.

[purpose]

Paul wrote this letter so that Philemon would accept his slave back without harsh punishment.

APPENDIX: PAUL'S MISSIONARY JOURNEYS

[paul's first missionary journey]

Acts 13	Antioch (Syria)	Lystra
	Seleucia	Derbe
	Cyprus (island)	Lystra
	-Salamis	Iconium
	-Paphos	Antioch (Pisidia)
	Antioch (Pisidia)	Perga
	Iconium	Seleucia

Acts 14	Antioch (Syria) - Galatians written
	Jerusalem Council

[paul's second missionary journey]

Acts 15	Antioch (Syria) 49 AD	Berea
	Derbe	Athens
	Lystra	Corinth - 1 & 2 Thessalonians written
	Iconium	Cenchrene
	Antioch (Pisidia)	Ephesus
	Troas	Caesarea
	Phillippi	Jerusalem
	Thessalonica	

Acts 18	Antioch (Syria) 52 AD

[paul's third missionary journey]

Antioch (Syria) 53 AD Greece	
Galatia & Phygia	Athens
Derbe	Corinth - Romans written
Lystra	Macedonia
Iconium	Troas
Antioch (Pisidia)	Miletus
Ephesus - 1 Corinthians written	Tyre
Macedonia	Caesarea
Phillippi	Jerusalem 57 AD
Thessalonica	
Berea	

[paul's journey to rome and both imprisonments]

Caesarea

Crete

Malta

Rome (house arrest) - Philemon, Colossians, Ephesians, & Philippians written

Macedonia - 1 Timothy written

Nicopolis - Titus written

Rome - 2 Timothy written

[appendix: chronology of paul's life]

AD 36	Paul's conversion
AD 45	Famine visit to Jerusalem
AD 46-48	First missionary journey
AD 49	Jerusalem council (Acts 15)
AD 50-52	Second missionary journey
AD 53-57	Third missionary journey
AD 57-60	Paul's arrest at Jerusalem; imprisonment at Caesarea
AD 61-63	First imprisonment in Rome
AD 63-66	Visits churches in Macedonia
AD 66-67	Second imprisonment in Rome
AD 68	Death of Paul

HEBREWS THROUGH REVELATION

ROOTED:NEW TESTAMENT

ROOTED:NEW TESTAMENT

study six hebrews through revelation

TABLE OF CONTENTS

INTRODUCTION

This final section will finish up our survey of the New Testament. This section will cover the General Letters and Revelation.

This section will cover:

- some of the basic characteristics of the epistle;

- a brief look at the authors who wrote this portion of the New Testament;

- a survey of each book, including recipients, structure, and themes.

THE ANCIENT LETTER

Note: This section on the epistles is essentially the same as in Lesson 5 in case you have students who missed that lesson.

Paul's writings aren't technically letters; they belong to a genre (type) of literature called an "**epistle**."

(a) Letter: private communication, written to one person.

(b) Epistle: public communication, more official, written to a group.

[some characteristics]

1. Epistles were common in the ancient world. They were generally written by a scribe called an "amanuensus." The author would normally **dictate** his letter to the scribe.

(a) This process usually isn't word for word; rather, the scribe **took notes** and wrote out the actual text at a later time.

(b) If the author was intending for his work to be circulated to many groups he would carefully **review** the final product.

2. The term epistle is used to describe a body of literature that fits into a similar **form** and structure. Aside from lengthening his epistles, Paul wrote them according to the same rules as his contemporaries:

(a) name of the **writer** and recipient;

Paul, a servant of Christ Jesus, called to be an apostle and set apart for the Gospel of God . . . . To all in Rome who are loved by God and called to be saints (Romans 1:1, 7a).

(b) some greeting wishing peace for the recipient;

Grace and peace to you from God our Father and from the Lord Jesus Christ (Romans 1:7b).

(c) polite expression of **thanks** for the good health for the recipient. Paul expanded this to give thanks to God;

First, I thank my God through Jesus Christ for all of you, because your faith is being reported all over the world (Romans 1:8).

(d) main body of letter (Paul's epistles are considerably **longer** than their ancient counterparts);

(e) personal **news**;

But now that there is no more place for me to work in these regions, and since I have been longing for many years to see you, I plan to do so when I go to Spain. I hope to visit you while passing through and to have you assist me on my journey there, after I have enjoyed your company for a while (Romans 15:23-24).

(f) exhortation or **blessing**;

I urge you, brothers, to watch out for those who cause divisions and put obstacles in your way that are contrary to the teaching you have learned. Keep away from them (Romans 16:17).

(g) ends with a word of farewell, which Paul usually expanded to a **prayer**.

Now to him who is able to establish you by my Gospel and the proclamation of Jesus Christ, according to the revelation of the mystery hidden for long ages past (Romans 16:25).

[reading the epistles]

1. The epistles were written to encourage and instruct believers at the **churches** he started.

2. They were read **publicly** and were intended for circulation amongst the surrounding churches.

3. They were written to a **specific audience** and, thus, addressed specific situations (occasion) for specific reasons (purpose).
   (a) Reading an epistle is like listening to one side of a phone conversation. Most of the conversation should be easy to understand, but some is difficult because we can't hear what the other person is **saying**. To add to the difficulties, we don't know what knowledge both sides share.

   (b) The Corinthians had different problems and questions than the Thessalonians, thus Paul wrote different letters to each group.

   (c) Because each epistle came out of a specific occasion, the writers had a specific **purpose** in each of their writings. There is a very close relationship between occasion and purpose.

4. Occasion and purpose are a bit harder to discover for the **General Letters**. We have little knowledge of the ministries of James, Peter, and John. With Paul's letters, we have the Book of Acts that provides a historical backdrop.

5. The epistles are not theological textbooks. Even Paul's "greatest" epistle, **Romans**, is not a textbook of systematic theology.

This means that no one letter holds "all the answers" about truth.
Understanding the entire context of a letter is all-important for good interpretation.

6. The New Testament writers always made a close connection between the theology of Christ and moral/ethical regulations (or ways of living) for the believer.

Head knowledge (theology or "beliefs about God") without application is worthless.

THE AUTHORS

[james]

1. James was a half brother to Jesus and an unbeliever during Jesus' life. According to 1 Corinthians 15:7, Jesus appeared to him **after** the resurrection.

In his letter, James calls himself a *"slave of God, and of the Lord Jesus Christ" (James 1:1 NLT)*. He makes no mention of being the brother of Jesus.

2. He was the **head** of the church in Jerusalem, referred to as one of the "pillars" of the church (Galatians 2:9). He probably didn't do very much traveling.

3. Early traditions teach that James was **stoned** to death for his faith (not to be confused by the James who was killed on Herod's orders by the sword in Acts 12:2).

4. One commentator has noted that James does not say very much about Jesus, but that his **words** sound very much like Jesus. Nearly everything James wrote has a parallel in one of the Gospels. (Lockyer, Herbert. *All the Apostles of the Bible*, page 198.)

[peter]

1. Peter was one of the original twelve disciples, and one of Jesus' three **closest** friends. The other two were James (not the James who wrote the letter) and John.

He grew up as a **fisherman** on the shores of the Sea of Galilee.
Peter is often characterized as blunt, impetuous, egotistical, and simple.

2. Peter was usually the disciple to speak first, and often too **quickly**.

From that time on Jesus began to explain to his disciples that he must go to Jerusalem and suffer many things at the hands of the elders, chief priests and teachers of the law, and that he must be killed and on the third day be raised to life. Peter took him aside and began to rebuke him. "Never, Lord!" he said. "This shall never happen to you!" Jesus turned and said to Peter, "Get behind me, Satan! You are a stumbling block to me; you do not have in mind the things of God, but the things of men" (Matthew 16:21-23).

3. Peter was with Jesus for nearly the entire three years of his ministry. The Gospels and Acts record numerous **significant** events in the life of Peter. A few highlights are:

- Peter is called to be an apostle (Luke 5).

- Jesus says, "upon this rock I'll build my church" (Matthew 16:18).

- Peter was at the transfiguration (Matthew 17:1-9).

- Peter walked on water to Jesus (Matthew 14:26-31).

- Jesus reinstated Peter after the resurrection (John 21:15-25).

- In the garden of Gethsemane, Peter cut off the ear of Malchus when Jesus was arrested (Luke 22:47-51).

- Peter preached for the first time on the day of Pentecost (Acts 2).

[john]

1. John was also one of the twelve disciples. He grew up in Galilee where his wealthy father owned several boats. John probably never knew **poverty** until he followed Jesus.

2. John the apostle was a follower of John the Baptist, who preached in the desert the repentance of sins and the arrival of the **Messiah**. When Jesus came, John the apostle followed Him.

3. John enjoyed a unique position among the disciples; he was clearly Jesus' closest and most **intimate** friend. John is often called the "disciple whom Jesus loved" (see John 13:23, 19:26, 20:2, 21:7, 21:20).

When Jesus was dying, He told John to look after His **mother** (John 19:26-27).

In humility, John never names himself in his Gospel.

4. John was apparently a leader in the church in Jerusalem, then in Ephesus. After that, he was **exiled** to the Isle of Patmos by the Romans because he was a believer.

[jude]

Not much is known about the identity of Jude. He calls himself a "brother of James," but doesn't tell us which James (Jude 1). If this James was the brother of Jesus, then Jude was also an **unbeliever** until after the resurrection.

THE LETTERS

[hebrews]

1. The epistle to the Hebrews is unique among the letters. It dives deep into Jewish **theology** and redefines it from the inside out, making Jesus the center.

Without a good foundation of knowledge about Old Testament history and teachings, Hebrews can be very difficult to understand.

2. The letter was probably directed to Jewish **believers**.

3. The author is **never named**, and there are no clear clues for a definitive answer. Tradition claimed Paul, but most scholars would agree this is unlikely because of the writing style and vocabulary.

Interestingly, the book of Hebrews, in the original language, is considered to be the most eloquent and well written book in the New Testament.

4. The structure of Hebrews is **easy** to follow because the author supplies several key words and phrases.

5. Major themes include:
- the superiority of Christ over angels, **Moses**, and the old priesthood;

- Jesus as the great high **priest**—mediator of a better covenant;

- great examples of **faithful** people of God;

- the **confidence** a believer has before God.

Therefore, since we are receiving a kingdom that cannot be shaken, let us be thankful, and so worship God acceptably with reverence and awe, for our "God is a consuming fire" (Hebrews 12:29).

[james]

1. James' letter is addressed to *the twelve tribes scattered among the nations . . . . believers in our glorious Lord Jesus Christ" (1:1, 2:1).* James clearly intended Jewish **Christians** to read his letter.

The history in the book of Acts records the persecution and scattering of the Christians in Jerusalem. The recipients of this letter were among those scattered and without leadership.

2. This letter does not emphasize the theological aspects of Christianity (although it is not empty of truth about God). Instead, James turns his attention to **practical** Christian living.

3. The message of James is similar to the teachings of Jesus in the Sermon on the Mount (Matthew 5-7) and **Proverbs**.

4. Major themes include:
- facing trials with **joy** and patience;

- listening and **obedience** walk hand-in-hand;

- favoritism breaks God's law;

- faith and deeds walk hand in hand;

- controlling the tongue;

- **humbleness** before God;

- prayer is always a good idea.

Therefore confess your sins to each other and pray for each other so that you may be healed. The prayer of a righteous man is powerful and effective (James 5:16).

[1 peter]

1. First Peter is addressed to *God's elect . . . scattered throughout (1:1)* and written to encourage and testify *that this is the true grace of God. Stand fast in it (5:12).* Peter did not write to a **single city** or region, but clearly intended his letter to be distributed.

2. This letter addresses common problems Christians were facing everywhere. Living in a pagan society where few knew God, the Christians were often misunderstood and faced **persecution**.

3. Peter's letter is pastoral; he wanted to extend his **sympathy** for their difficult situations and offer advice on how to survive.

4. Major themes include:
   - salvation: **plan** and responsibilities included;

   - submission: Christian **duty** to authority;

   - suffering: what happens when Christians live a **holy** life;

   - sanctification: **process** through which Christians become more like Christ.

You also, like living stones, are being built into a spiritual house to be a holy priesthood, offering spiritual sacrifices acceptable to God through Jesus Christ (1 Peter 2:5).

[2 peter]

1. The exact recipients of 2 Peter cannot clearly be determined. The letter is addressed to **believers** without mention of location. Second Peter 3:1 refers to a former letter. If this is a reference to 1 Peter, then we can assume 2 Peter was directed to the same audience.

Although we can't be sure who the initial readers were, Peter's pastoral intent is clear: to give *reminders to stimulate you to wholesome thinking (3:1).*

2. There are many similarities between 2 Peter and Jude (compare 2 Peter with Jude 4-18). Many believe one **borrowed** from the other, or that both used a common source.

3. Although this letter is short (3 chapters), its message is still important. Some major themes include:
   - the call for spiritual **maturity**;

   - prophecy is a reality because it comes from **God**;

   - warnings against **false** teachers;

   - waiting for the coming Day of the Lord.

The Lord is not slow in keeping his promise, as some understand slowness. He is patient with you, not wanting anyone to perish, but everyone to come to repentance (2 Peter 3:9).

[1 john]

1. First John was written to believers, although it lacks a specific name of a particular community. Internal evidence suggests there was **division** within the Christian community, and John wrote this letter to reaffirm the truth about Christian community.

2. The beliefs of the "other" community were an early form of Gnosticism, a mixture of Greek philosophy and **Christianity**.

The Gnostics believed and taught the following:
  - physical things are **evil**, God is pure spirit, which is good;

  - salvation comes through having the right **knowledge**, or secret wisdom;

  - Jesus wasn't fully God, only an "emanation" of God;

  - Jesus was good, and didn't have a physical **body**;

  - because the body was evil, this led to either self-indulgence or self-**mutilation**.

3. John re-established basic Christian beliefs, and taught that true knowledge is reflected in one's **lifestyle**.

Some of the major themes include:
  - God is seen as the Light, righteousness, and **love**;

  - no one is without **sin**;

  - warnings against antichrists;

  - believers are the **children** of God; loving God is followed by obedience;

  - Jesus was the God-man, who suffered to save the world;

  - salvation is **secure** and certain for believers.

I write these things to you who believe in the name of the Son of God so that you may know that you have eternal life (1 John 5:13).

[2 john]

1. The 13 verses of this letter are addressed "To the chosen lady and her children." Scholars are divided in their treatment of this verse. Some believe this letter is written to an actual person. Others believe this address to be a **metaphor** for a church community.

2. In the early days of the Church, wandering teachers spread the Gospel. Christian communities were to welcome them into their homes and provide them with food, shelter, etc. False teachers also made use of their hospitality **to spread lies**.

3. Major themes in this letter include:
   - loving one another means **obedience** to God's commands;

   - warning against **welcoming** false teachers, as doing so helps them.

And this is love: that we walk in obedience to his commands. As you have heard from the beginning, his command is that you walk in love (2 John 6).

[3 john]

1. The 13 verses of 3 John are addressed to Gaius. This letter also deals with Christian hospitality with traveling **missionaries**. John encourages Gaius to be faithful in the work he is doing for the brothers, even though they were "strangers" to him.

2. One church leader (Diotrephes) was neglecting his duty of **hospitality** and even excluding Christians from the church fellowship for welcoming missionaries.

Dear friend, do not imitate what is evil but what is good. Anyone who does what is good is from God. Anyone who does what is evil has not seen God (3 John 11).

[jude]

1. The letter from Jude is addressed to believers in general, although he deals with a very specific problem. Jude wrote "about the salvation we share . . . to contend for the faith that was once for all entrusted to the saints" (v. 3). Due to the heavy use of Old Testament **history**, the readers were probably Jewish.

2. In only 25 verses, Jude's arguments are clear and to the point. The church to which he was writing was **infected** by false teachers who had *secretly slipped in* and changed *the grace of our God into a license for immorality (v. 4)*.

3. These false teachers were immoral, living self-indulgent lives, and opposing the **truth**.

4. Some major themes include:
  - warnings against false teachers;

  - examples from Jewish **history**: unbelieving Israel, fallen angels, and Sodom and Gomorrah;

  - the call to build up in the **faith**.

But you, dear friends, build yourselves up your most holy faith and pray in the Holy Spirit (Jude 20).

[revelation]

1. The Book of Revelation stands **alone** in the New Testament as its own style, although it's technically an epistle written to seven churches (five of the seven had major problems).

Among Christians, no other teaching or text creates more controversy debate, and confusion.

> **THE SEVEN CHURCHES:**
> Revelation is addressed to seven ancient churches. John praised them for their faithfulness. He also called them on their mistakes:
>
> Ephesus
>   -Lost their first love
> Smyrna
>   -No criticism
> Pergamum
>   -Following false teachers
> Thyatira
>   -Tolerating immorality
> Sardis
>   -Spiritually asleep
> Philadelphia
>   -No criticism
> Laodicea
>   -Ineffective with their faith

2. Revelation is unique in the way it teaches God's Truth. One doesn't need to read far before fantastic imagery is found. The language and symbolism are difficult for the modern reader to understand. Did God intentionally **choose** to make His message obscure? Or, could the original intended readers understand it?

It was not **difficult** for the original readers, they were familiar with literature which used imagery like that found in Revelation.

The truth Revelation teaches **requires** imagery. John is giving us a tiny view of Heaven and the future. Revelation is not alone in its use of imagery; Jesus used parables to describe the Kingdom of Heaven.

Many have noted a strong connection between John's language and imagery in Revelation and the Old Testament book of Daniel. One who is familiar with **Daniel** will be well equipped to understand Revelation.

3. Scholars normally structure Revelation one of two ways:

   (a) By **Events**: seven churches (chapters 2–3); seven seals (6–8); seven trumpets (8–11); seven signs (12–15); seven bowls (15–18); seven last things (19–22)

   (b) By **Visions**: (1) the Son of man among the seven churches (chapters 1–3); (2) the seven-sealed scroll, the seven trumpets, the seven signs, and the seven bowls (4:1–19:10); (3) the return of Christ and the consummation of this age (19:11–20:15); (4) the new Heaven and new earth (21–22).

4. Another unique element of Revelation is found in its use of the Old Testament. Although there are no direct quotations, in the 404 verses of Revelation, **278** contain references to the Old Testament.

5. One common pitfall to the interpretation of Revelation is focusing on **prophecy** and not on Jesus Christ.

Although readers are called, *"Blessed is the one who reads the words of this prophecy (1:3),"* a person must be careful not to forget Jesus' warning in Acts 1:7: *"It is not for you to* **know** *the times or dates the Father has set by his own authority."*

6. There are four major ways to understand and interpret Revelation:

Futurist:
Everything in Revelation describes the future, specifically, events preceding and following the **return** of Jesus. This view holds that no events described in Revelation have happened yet.

Historicist:
This view sees Revelation as describing historical events beginning with the time of the **apostles**. Thus many of the events described have already occurred. There is not much agreement among scholars on how specific passages in Revelation correspond to historical events.

Preterist:
This view sees the entire book of Revelation as a description of events **only** within John's time. This means everything described in Revelation has already happened.

Idealist:
Revelation is seen as poetry, symbolic, and spiritual in nature. This view finds a spiritual lesson in every verse, and sees Revelation as having nothing to do with actual **history**.

7. Ultimately, John was a pastor, and he wrote Revelation to encourage and correct the churches. Not only did they need to correct their **behavior**, but they needed to know the hope that God will one day defeat evil. Life was difficult (and still is). Without hope it is impossible. The devil won't exist forever, Jesus will return for His church, and believers will live eternally in Heaven. The central purpose of Revelation is to communicate a message of **hope**.

Then I saw a new heaven and a new earth, for the first heaven and the first earth had passed away, and there was no longer any sea. I saw the Holy City, the new Jerusalem, coming down out of heaven from God, prepared as a bride beautifully dressed for her husband. And I heard a loud voice from the throne saying, "Now the dwelling of God is with men, and he will live with them. They will be his people, and God himself will be with them and be their God. He will wipe every tear from their eyes. There will be no more death or mourning or crying or pain, for the old order of things has passed away" (Revelation 21:1-4).